Care

Síreacht: Longings for Another Ireland is a series of short, topical and provocative texts on controversial issues in contemporary Ireland.

Contributors to the *Síreacht* series come from diverse backgrounds and perspectives but share a commitment to the exposition of what may often be disparaged as utopian ideas, minority perspectives on society, polity and environment, or critiques of received wisdom. Associated with the phrase *ceól sírechtach síde* found in Irish medieval poetry, *síreacht* refers to yearnings such as those evoked by the music of the *aos sí*, the supernatural people of Irish mythology. As the title for this series, we use it to signify longings for and imaginings of a better world in the spirit of the World Social Forums that 'another world is possible'. At the heart of the mythology of the *sí* is the belief that lying beneath this world is the other world. So too these texts address the urgent challenge to imagine potential new societies and relationships, but also to recognise the seeds of these other worlds in what already exists.

Other published titles in the series are

Freedom? by Two Fuse
Public Sphere by Harry Browne
Commemoration by Heather Laird
Money by Conor McCabe
Self by Eilís Ward
Sexual/Liberation by Michael G. Cronin
Trade Unions by Adrian Kane

The editors of the series, Órla O'Donovan, Fiona Dukelow, Rosie Meade, School of Applied Social Studies and Heather Laird, School of English, University College Cork, welcome suggestions or proposals for consideration as future titles in the series. Please see http://sireacht.ie/ for more information.

Care

MARK GARAVAN

Series Editors:

Órla O'Donovan, Fiona Dukelow,
Rosie Meade and Heather Laird

CORK UNIVERSITY PRESS

First published in 2024 by
Cork University Press
Boole Library
University College Cork
Cork T12 ND89
Ireland

Library of Congress number: 2024930324

British Library Cataloguing in Publication Data
A CIP catalogue record for this book is available from the British
Library.

ISBN 9781782056119

Typeset by Studio 10 Design
Printed by Hussar Books in Poland

Cover image © Shutterstock.com

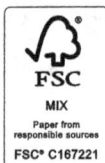

FSC

MIX

Paper from
responsible sources

FSC® C167221

CONTENTS

*This book is dedicated to those
I care for the most –
Pauline, Eve and Stephen.*

Acknowledgements

No book is the product of one person, and this one least of all. The ideas outlined here have been developed from countless experiences, conversations, meetings and exchanges from when I first entered Dublin Simon Community as a volunteer worker over thirty-five years ago in 1988. I have been their receiver, not their originator. I particularly appreciate the many students of social care that I have worked with since 2008 in ATU Mayo, and more recently the insights and honesty of peer support students. I am indebted to all of them. The many discussions I have had in Mayo Recovery College have been particularly enriching and have given me access to worlds often hidden and marginal such as those of voice hearers. I would like to record a special thanks to those many individuals I have come to know who have found a way to be courageously human in an often careless world. I will here name two only – Jutta Kirkham and Kathy Mayock. Finally, I am deeply grateful to the editors of the *Síreacht* series for their careful and respectful reading. The book has greatly benefited from their helpful suggestions but all content and defects are my responsibility.

The Problem with Care

When we think about 'care' we may initially be tempted to view it as a reasonably straightforward concept. After all, we each experience care both as care givers and care receivers. It is a practice that appears to be natural. Yet, when we investigate it, it transforms into a rather more elusive notion than we may have expected. For example, when might practising care slip into doing harm? If my care for you is overly focused on protecting you from injury, might I end up by depriving you of autonomy? Or when might care become a method of control? A family member whose emotional pain causes them to behave in ways that are upsetting to others may well benefit from medication but, once again, is there a threshold where prolonged medication becomes a regime of chemical repression?

Is care about holding and minding someone or is it about letting go and freeing them? Can one learn to care? Can one care better? Is care a feeling linked to states of empathy or compassion or is it better understood as a decision, or a commitment to another person? Is care solely located in the inter-personal realm or does it necessarily include the socio-political also? Can I fully care for a person who is wheelchair-bound if I do not also campaign for physical and access changes in the world of social space? Might certain practices of care be an impediment to genuine well-being if they are confined to addressing symptoms of social ills rather than causes?

Is care something that only occurs between human beings? Does it not also include relations with animals, especially social animals like pets? But what about domestic animals used in farming and for food? Are they cared for? What about places, habitats, trees, rivers? Do we not in fact exhibit great care for other-than-human life forms? What about care for abstract human conceptions such as nations, football teams, art? What about spiritual beings?

When we contemplate the practice of care in our lived experiences it seems to be deeply embedded into our very humanity. This makes care difficult to disentangle from our wider human involvements and to therefore examine as a discrete concept. Such a task becomes all the more difficult when we recognise that our notions and practices of care are also shaped by prevailing ideological norms. These norms become the taken-for-granted features of a habituated cultural reproduction and social practice.

The building in Castlebar, County Mayo, where I work as a social care academic serves well to illustrate this. It was built as a district lunatic asylum and opened in 1866, catering initially for 162 people. In its time it was seen as providing a very progressive, modern form of care to those then judged as 'insane'. Rather than the mentally distressed being confined to their homes, or sent to wander abroad at potential risk to themselves and possibly a disturbance to others, the establishment of a structured, clean and provisioned institution of care was widely regarded as a positive development. Extensions were added in 1878, 1882, 1902 and 1936. An inscription stone still visible on the façade of the building dated to 1934 describes it as *Teach na nGealt* or madhouse. It was a classical Victorian institution of care, with sombre grey stone, narrow corridors to control circulation and movement, and a large perimeter fence to ensure the confinement of its inmates. Like many such in the wide array of Irish nineteenth- and early twentieth-century institutions, its purported and no doubt well-intentioned provision of care was nonetheless closely allied with the task of control of those categorised as deviant and socially disruptive.

The Census records of 1901 show a total of 723 persons resident, 288 of them female.[1] They are recorded using only their initials. The Census lists the 'kind of insanity' under which they were detained as well as giving the 'presumed cause of insanity'. The diagnostic labels were mostly dementia and chronic mania, with a smaller number noted as melancholia. For the most part the causes were listed as unknown but the range of assumed causes that were suggested would no doubt strike the contemporary reader as suspect if not downright dubious. These included religious excitement, heredity, insomnia, softening of brain, disappointment, trouble, discharge from army, poverty, fright, shock, sunstroke, jealousy, immoral habits, drink, masturbation.

By the 1950s there were approximately 1,300 residents. The walls around the building were removed in 1963 and from the 1980s the complex was slowly emptied of its residents in favour of the new de-institutionalisation model of smaller houses in more community settings. The end of the confinement regime was in turn heralded as the dawn of a new, modern and progressive form of care. The assumption was that an oppressive care practice had now given way to genuine care.

The transition of the building seemed to symbolise this transformation. In 1994 a portion of the building was given over to enable a campus of the newly established Galway-Mayo Regional Technical College to be formed. This campus expanded to include a greater portion of the building and the college itself underwent further corporate change, becoming the Galway-Mayo Institute of Technology and, more recently, the Atlantic Technological University.

In time, the campus has specialised in providing degrees in health and social care professional practice on programmes such as General Nursing, Mental Health Nursing, Social Care, Early Childhood Care and Education, and Peer Support Practice. In an unexpected way, the building had evolved from a site of institutionalised care to one of professionalised training. As Foucault observed in *The Order of Discourse*,[2] each approach armed itself with supporting knowledge claims, systems of verification and rationality, structures of reproduction, and a panoply of surveillance criteria to determine orthodoxy from heresy. The practitioner successfully socialised within each model has few grounds to doubt or dispute their fundamental veracity. However, as we will examine below, the structure of professionalised health and social care is itself no longer fit for use and it too, like institutionalisation before it, is no longer adequate in responding to the complex demands of our time.

If this is true and, given the range of questions I have posed above, how do we proceed to make sense of care for twenty-first-century Ireland? How might we outline a care model that is genuinely viable and progressive? How might we imagine care for a new Ireland? Various reports (and their attendant apologies) into Ireland's grim history of institutional care, particularly *The Ryan Report* (2009) and *The McAleese Report* (2013) into the Magdalene laundries, may have misled us into a complacency that the end of confinement and coercive care has brought about a new era of person-centred, non-judgemental care provision ('that was then, this is now'). Instead, old problems have been replaced with new problems, and old dysfunctions of neglect have been replaced with new dysfunctions of neglect. The failures of one's own time may simply be more difficult to perceive given the power of the ideological framing and its attendant socialisation to lure and lull.

This book sets out to re-think and re-imagine care for an Ireland facing the unprecedented challenges of the present century. It offers a possible model for our system of care grounded on principles of dialogue and seeks to resituate the wider practice of care as an activity of commoning. The dialogic model of care is complemented by the proposal for a universal basic income to better support the caring commons. The imperative to do this comes from the recognition that we have entered a time of crisis and breakdown. This is manifesting itself right across our economic and political systems. In this wider disintegration, our forms of professional care practice are necessarily implicated. Indeed, the very extent of growing systemic failure will impose insuperable burdens on a care structure increasingly incapable of adequate response. In addition, the status and practice of care as an activity of the human commons is also under threat and pressure. For many, our world is increasingly experienced as lacking care, as a harsh and tough arena characterised by competition and isolation. The figure of the wall has emerged as a literal and metaphoric image demarcating the zones of winners and losers, of the cared-for and the uncared-for. The 'sacrifice zones' of global capitalism seem to require a martyrdom of care itself.[3]

The great difficulty that we have is that at this very moment of crisis (both in the sense of peril and opportunity for change) when we require a collective response, our ideological apparatuses have summoned up an almost entrancing depiction of human autonomy, centred on the claim that each individual is sovereign and can make whatever choices they wish based on their own unique desires. This assertion within liberal humanism that the goal of life is self-actualisation manifested in personal choice and unlimited freedom has been deeply magnified by two powerful social forces of the late twentieth century. These are neoliberalism with its elevation of the self-interested rational actor who must find their way in a competitive marketplace (a concept now extended to most areas of human life) and the subsequent technological turbocharging of self-referential subjectivity through the advent of social media and the wider internet. The amalgam of the thinking framework of neoliberalism with the enabling infrastructure of the internet has propelled many western humans into an all-encompassing enclosure of private desire. The superego demand of today is that personal happiness is the ultimate good. Its achievement is primarily attained through individually tailored consumption. While in the best of times this claim to the good life may be curious and perhaps harmless for the rest of humanity and life on Earth, this is not the best of times. Indeed, as has been said, it may well be the worst of times.

Thus, we appear particularly ill-equipped to respond to the reality of the world before us. Weighed down and distracted by competing post-modernisms, endless contestation, and the loss of collective structures of meaning, we seem to be disarmed of the means to address the unfolding tragedy of our times. Our century has already seen economic collapse in the privileged centre, a global pandemic, state health mandates in liberal societies restricting numerous social freedoms, global refugee crises, climate breakdown with droughts, floods, fires and extreme heat events, democratic fragility in the United States and elsewhere, and more recently, war returned to continental Europe. In the face of all these disruptive events it is not surprising to see the yearning for old certainties such as nationalism, ethno-centrism and populist demagoguery of right and left.

It does not seem too unreasonable to propose that at such a time we need the re-affirmation of care as a supporting foundation for human well-being. This book seeks to respond to this specific challenge and to explore how we might re-imagine a viable model of care for twenty-first-century Ireland. At the core of this proposal will be an attempt to recover a conceptualisation of care that moves beyond its modernist expressions in confinement and control, professionalism and commodity, and instead relocates care as a practice of the commons. This is, however, a short book so it necessarily will draw broad brushstrokes and propose generalised suggestions.[4] What is lost in nuance and detail is, I hope, gained in the evocation of new possibilities. It is, in the classic sense, an *essay*, an attempt, not a rigorous analysis. We are, after all, in a deep malaise and paralysis of care. In saying this, however, I need to clarify at the outset that this judgement does not refer to individual human beings, those who are either professional or domestic care givers. Rather, I am explicitly referring to the *systemic* problem we are in which obliges otherwise good people to behave in ways that may not always be objectively caring. Our problem is not a failure of personal compassion but of external disruption of the natural bonds of care and solidarity between people. Indeed, I will argue as we proceed that our ideological apparatus and its resultant institutional expression is obscuring this natural human tendency to care (the caring commons) and, furthermore, is in fact rendering invisible 'actually existing' human care. In simple terms, we have constructed before us as ideal types the solitary hero, the achiever, the entrepreneur (often masculinised), rather than figures drawn from the domain of the intimate, the nurturing, the gentle. The brute social demarcation of winners and losers calibrates an orientation towards the achiever rather than the giver.

It is far easier to critique than to propose, and the concern of this book as part of the wider *Síreacht* series is to set out new ideas for modern Ireland. In suggesting a new way for care to be actualised I will attempt to move in two directions. First, in Towards a Reformed Care System, I will offer a new architecture of social care delivery centred on the primacy of a dialogic practice. In particular, I will utilise a model of care called *The Hologram* which I present simply as one viable example of a dialogically centred care model. I will scale this model up using the very modalities of performance measurement employed by neoliberal care regimes. This is to achieve an immediately applicable reform and transformation of the current system into something far more radical and accessible. I do this to avoid overly idealistic yearning for the unattainable perfect and so ensure that our feet are firmly on the ground of the possible. Secondly, though, in The Commons of Care, I briefly go beyond a concern with the care system and explore how we might re-animate the caring commons by freeing up resources of time and creativity through the device of a universal basic income. Our modern experience of living in a 'careless world' is not simply the consequence of a deficit of professional care resources but a deep loss of social and ecological *connection*. How might we reach beyond the confinement of the isolated individual towards a collective response to human and other-than-human suffering? Universal basic income may offer one means to restore our social commons.

In proceeding, I need to be explicit in my commitment to the core value and practice of dialogue. Dialogue is not just a method or a mode of practice. Rather, it describes a way of being human, of affirming genuine subjectivity (our unique perspective and claims) against the objectifications of contemporary institutions and utilitarian rationalities, a way of joining together with others in solidarity, and a pathway to discover reality and shape it. In claiming this, I don't wish to elevate dialogue as some unquestioned formula, nor as a normative panacea, but, on the contrary, I want to more modestly propose that proceeding dialogically is simply the optimum way to address our messy, contentious, human materiality while preserving the dignity and uniqueness of each person within a participative and democratic public sphere. After all, what might the alternative be? Rule by an elite of the wealthy, the expert, the enlightened? Rather than an assertion of superiority, dialogue acknowledges the partial, the uncertain, the tentative, the social. Crucially for my purposes here, dialogue will encompass the understanding of care which I will explore, which is that care is primarily a response to the need of the other. My argument is that the quality of care is precisely determined by the quality of our response to an other. The two movements of dialogue – listen and reply – are, in my view, correlated directly to the dynamics of care itself – cry and response. Unravelling all of this will form much of the substance of this short text. I devote The Dialogic Solution to a fuller discussion of dialogue and dialogic practice.

But let us begin with some context. Why do I say there is a crisis of care and how is this crisis manifested? Let me take each of the two dimensions of care that I'm addressing in turn – the care system and the caring commons. First, our formal care system is suffering a catastrophic deficit of capacity. In a scene from Woody Allen's movie *Annie Hall*, two women are complaining about the poor quality of food in a restaurant when one of them adds critically, 'And such small portions!' The issue with modern care in Ireland strangely echoes this. The problem is not an uncaring intention by institutions of care nor that we have uncaring professionals. As I have noted above, the challenge is structural, not personal. At its core, the fundamental issue is that the *capacity* to deliver meaningful and sufficient care is under assault.

From the perspective of professional social and health care, the primary problem is that our care needs are outstripping our care resources. Given this deficit, what resources are available are rationed and commodified for distribution within the quasi-market systems of current care delivery. We want care but there simply is not enough. Our needs are growing and so this gap is widening. The widening gap is creating yet more need which, in turn, puts even further pressure on care resources. It is not that professional care workers are less responsive than before. They are simply overwhelmed and disempowered, and largely unable to respond effectively to the growing needs before them.

So, we have a classic scarcity issue – too great a demand (care needs), too small a supply (care responses). In the domain of scarcity, the dominant ideological reflex is set by a neoliberal paradigm which posits ever more stringent market disciplines as the best way to efficiently allocate resources within the constricted care market.[5] Thus, the delivery of care becomes marketised and commodified to deal with the scarcity challenge.

I will assess this issue more deeply in The Dialogic Solution and examine how this paradigm is impacting on care delivery. For now, let me merely note some empirical indicators of this scarcity challenge. These are taken from a cursory survey of news reports.

The Irish Times on 13 May 2023, citing figures from the National Treatment Purchase Fund, reported that more than 830,000 patients were waiting to be seen at an outpatient clinic or waiting for hospital treatment.[6] Almost 500,000 were waiting longer than the recommended Sláintecare maximum waiting time. In February 2023, RTÉ News reported that twenty-three out of twenty-eight hospitals had longer waiting lists in December 2022 than in December 2019.[7] On 15 June 2022 RTÉ News reported figures showing the over-burden in the accident and emergency system.[8] The average waiting time for treatment was more than eleven hours.

As of August 2023, the Mental Health Commission reported that 4,450 children were on the CAMHS (Child and Adolescent Mental Health Services) waiting list.[9] A survey reported the previous year had shown the number waiting had increased by a quarter in one year, with 10 per cent of these waiting longer than twelve months.[10]

While people may be on waiting lists, pain and emotions do not wait. They continue and, if untreated, likely escalate in severity.

> Disability organisations are calling on the urgent implementation of interim measures to address the lack of services being provided to children with disabilities following the stark findings of two recent surveys. Over 50% of the families of children surveyed by Inclusion Ireland were not in receipt of any service. Another survey by Down Syndrome Ireland backs this finding with almost half of their respondents reporting no therapy of any kind in the last year. Many parents reported that their child spent a significant time on a waiting list for services. 85% of the Inclusion Ireland respondents said that they have waited or continue to wait for more than a year, with some waiting more than six years.[11]

Statistic after statistic can be cited here. They will all show the same disturbing picture – the demand for care services greatly outstrips the supply. When one adds in Ireland's demographic profile the situation is even more foreboding. According to the 2016 Census, 'age dependency', which is measured as the number of younger (0–14) and older (65+) people as a percentage of those of working age (15–64), increased from 49.3 per cent in 2011 to 52.7 per cent in 2016. The number in the '65 and over' category increased by 102,174 to 637,567 – a rise of more than twice the 15–64 age category, which rose by 44,477 since 2011.[12]

If we add to this picture the effects of current and future pandemics, the impact of global migration, the escalating cost of medical and care resources and the yet unknown impacts of climate breakdown, then the picture does not look very positive. Indeed, it is also necessary to pay attention to the multiple indicators of poverty and social inequality which are the key determinants of health status and therefore of care needs. For example, by the summer of 2022 it was reported that almost one third of Irish people were experiencing fuel poverty.[13] It is entirely reasonable to predict that care needs will continue to escalate.

If this is the 'demand' side, then the 'supply' side also seems bleak. The very challenging working environment for health and social care professionals has led to significant recruitment and retention problems.[14] The professional registration of social care workers in Ireland under the auspices of CORU has been accompanied by the fragmentation of care worker grades and a growing reliance on relief staff.[15] Employers have no requirement or incentive to employ registered social care workers who simply add to their costs when the same work can be done by more temporary, lower-qualified staff on lower pay rates.

The consequence is that many people needing formal care cannot receive it, or at least, cannot receive it adequately.[16] One way that we might be able to get a sense of the lived experience of this supply reduction is through the prism of time. In the past, a feature of institutionalised care was the control of time and space. Time was highly regulated by routines and schedules. In the institutional setting everything was done in an orderly way driven in part by a belief that a high level of structure was of inherent benefit to someone whose mind and behaviours were 'dis-ordered'. Today, in professionalised social care, time is controlled by being rationed and valued in monetary terms. This is why we have waiting lists – there simply is not enough professional care time to go around. All needs cannot be met.

Yet, for the work of care to be done, time is needed. This is because, at a minimum, care is fundamentally a question of relationship – of a qualitative interaction between human beings. Time is therefore our most important care resource but today our systems of care do not have time to give freely. It is not that care workers do not care in a subjective sense. It is that they do not have sufficient time to give as a care resource. Today, the most subversive thing you can do is to publicly 'waste' time. The ability to waste time is almost impossible in a modern work environment, including a care work environment, structured as it is by outcome metrics, key performance indicators, targets and strategic outcomes.

Specifically in the case of care work, the queue of human need obliges you to move along at pace. It is impossible to dwell caringly with an individual when the implication is less or no time with another. Again, it is important to stress that the failure of care today is not a personal failure – it is systemic. We have largely an industrial caring system modelled on business practices. In such a system relationship gives way to utility, dialogue to function, the human subject requiring response becomes an object to be worked upon. In a world of objects, the figure of the discarded, the unwanted, the unvalued looms inevitably into view.

The second dimension of care that I wish to address is the care experienced and exchanged within the non-marketised and non-commodified realm of the personal – what we may designate as the caring commons. I will define and discuss the concept of the commons, particularly the caring commons, in The Commons of Care. For the purposes of this book, my concern with the commons is its characteristic as the realm of dialogic relationship, that is of inter-subjective response, operating outside the regime of capitalist commodification and neoliberal surveillance. It seems evident that our default human state is that of interdependence.[17] We live necessarily within the shelter and support of mutual relations. Professional care simply cannot replace these connections. Yet our communal connections are being eroded. This is one of the engines driving further the gap between care need and care provision. The loss of social connections in turn creates new forms of emerging care needs resulting from loneliness, isolation and existential marginalisation. New types of addiction can be observed characteristic of the solitary being, such as to virtual reality, computer gaming, online pornography.

Much care labour, indeed the vast majority of actual care, is done within families and within homes, mostly by women. Often, this care is socially invisible and un-acknowledged. Our evolutionary advantage as a species lay in our capacity to develop co-operative care. In this way the very young and the very old could be nurtured and sustained in life. However, we in the West no longer live in extended family or communal settings but in vast modern states. The erosion of personal and familial connections characteristic of the western world has forced us into greater reliance on social care systems. But, as I have said, we live at a time when these systems of care are breaking down. Indeed, today, the very appeal to the social, to solidarity, seems suspect. Rather, the responsibilised individual is privileged.

The modern family is a very battered and bruised entity. Though it is the locus of primary socialisation and of fundamental care with lifelong implications for health and well-being, any assertion of the intrinsic value of the family (irrespective of the empirical diversity of its contemporary forms) is now embroiled in our culture-war contestations. The ideological elevation of individualism has diluted the normative value of family formation in any of its varied modes. All families in their pluriform expressions are subject to intense economic pressures regarding attaining home ownership, domestic task management and work commuting. In such a situation, it is not surprising that much of the care labour of the family must be outsourced to childminders, pre-school settings, home care workers and nursing homes (much of which is done by poorer and precariously employed women). Once again, it is structural forces which are re-ordering how the family can perform. The universal basic income proposal explored in this book attempts to better resource families in the task of care and to free individual family carers from economic dependency on higher-income family members or from being obliged to undertake low-paid, precarious employment. This should make the distribution of domestic care roles more a matter of decision than of obligation.

As I will explore further in this book, the consumer capitalist culture of gratification, self-realisation through consumption, and the elevation of the autonomous self renders questionable social values that are essential to doing care, such as sacrifice and relegating one's own needs to that of another. When these forces are allied to the patriarchal view of care as woman's work and of lower status than the public work of men, then we have a deep undermining of the caring commons.

The implications of these opening ideas need to be further teased out and elaborated. For now, I wish only to propose that our society is engaged in a type of burning the candle at both ends. On one end, the neoliberal ascendency in modern Ireland is constructing ever more atomised individuals with ever greater care requirements. The ecological and social dislocations of liberal capitalism are in turn creating new and emerging care needs. On the other end, the rationality of neoliberalism has led to care being conceptualised as a scarce service within a market that therefore must be rationed in accordance with financial and welfare capacities. In short, it is the combination of these demand and supply factors which results in our crisis of care. However, crisis is not just potential breakdown. It is also a potential break-through and it is into that territory that this short book is seeking to venture. The objective is not only to move from our institutionalised care paradigm of the past with its focus on *confinement* but also to go beyond the professionalised care paradigm of the present with its focus on *commodity*. Instead, out of the very crisis and the care deficit before us, I will explore models that centre on a peer-led care paradigm with a reliance on care as *commons*.

In so uncertain a situation, I want at the outset to claim two characteristics of care that might serve as foundations for our new model – care as an essential attribute of the commons and the materiality of care. The first is that the 'resource' of care – its practice, its very emergence as a human behaviour – is unequivocally a matter of the commons. I am here using the term commons in the sense of the vast labour of care performed outside of professional work or commodity exchange. As interdependent beings we require a relational exchange of care. In our life cycles we both receive care and give care. Our fragile human lives begin in receiving care. Without this we literally could not survive. If we live long enough, we will inevitably require care once again.

The second assumption I am making is the sheer materiality of care. Care is not an abstract matter. Our search for care does not emerge from our minds. It is not quite like the search for beauty or justice. Care emerges out of our very physical and embodied vulnerability. Irrespective of politics, identity or ideology, the human body is a site of physical need that breaks through our illusions of autonomy and symbolic, technological dis-embodiment. Birth, death, illness, with the attendant presence of smell, sweat, fluid, sound, obliges us to make a physical response to the vulnerable other and to our own vulnerability also. A baby's cry simply must be attended to. A person falling beside me simply must be reached out to. The pain and suffering of another cannot but evoke a response in me. If this were not so, then human beings would not survive the conditions of planet Earth. At the highest levels of sensibility, without empathy – the capacity to feel the feelings of another – our literature and art could not have developed.

Each of us is tied to a physical dependency on the caring other. We need other people. There is no way around this material corporeality. None of us could be alive without the receipt of vast amounts of care in our infancy and childhood. Our dying lies before us, but we know that human beings do not abandon the ill to die alone or discard their corpses as so much debris. Rather, we attend to each other's needs not as the result of some calculus of self-interest but because doing so is profoundly rooted in our human physical selves. It is in this specific sense that the activity of care is 'natural' for us – it is intrinsically bound up in the reciprocal reliance that we have with each other. This is why overt transgressions of care – violence, abandonment of the ill, desecration of the dead – cause us such profound distress. The twentieth century's dominant image of horror remains the concentration camp where these deviant features were exhibited to the full. Human beings are clearly capable of wanton carelessness but only in very specific conditions where the bonds of inter-subjectivity are forcibly ruptured or ideologically obscured.[18]

The implication of the materiality of care extends further in that the care-seeking disabled person – whether that disability be of mind or body, be temporary or permanent – subverts our ideological illusion of the sovereign self. Not all selves can be autonomous and 'rational' and self-interested. Are they to be excluded from our standards of the human subject? Clearly not. Yet the very presence of the 'disabled' other challenges us to respond with care rather than dismissal. As we will see below, the hegemonic notion of the human subject is drawn far too narrowly. Having to respond to the demands of care draws us out of ourselves and towards the other whose very corporeality requires of us a response. In this sense, we are interpellated by the presence of the other who requires care and this very request can (and indeed does) penetrate the illusion of the neoliberal subjectivity of the autonomous sovereign self. A similar revealing occurs if the individual themselves becomes dependent on others.

Building on these two assumptions, the argument of the book is that we need to initiate a paradigm shift in care from institutionalisation and professionalisation to a new commoning of care. It does this by proposing the activation of primarily peer-to-peer care networks grounded in dialogic practice, which on the one hand permits the individual person to access necessary support and help, and on the other hand organically constructs from the bottom up an invigorated culture of care. These networks can be mobilised and supported through the device of a universal basic income, which frees people from low-paid and precarious employment, economically rewards the actual work they do, and reduces the dependency and marginalisation of non-marketised carers. Thus, both the care system and the care commons are addressed. Such a cultural change serves to contest the dominant neoliberal framing of human subjectivity, which has contributed to our profoundly careless society. This proposed model draws generally on dialogic practices originating from Paulo Freire and others and, more specifically for exemplary purposes, on ideas developed by the feminist artist Cassie Thornton. By proposing dialogic care networks threaded within our fractured world, the text seeks to imagine and show how to practically actualise human connection and social change, and recover a social realm marked by conviviality and genuine care. Such a commons relies not on structure or institution but on bonds of mutuality between vulnerable embodied beings. The objective is to chart a clear course towards the realisation of the caring, and cared-for, human subject. What we are trying to escape is the careless world of isolated eco-psycho disintegration. What we are trying to find is the attentive response attained best from those happy to hear us and to bear us. This after all is the very feature that makes us human.

Of course, not everything about care can be said in any one text. The focus therefore will be on proposing an enhanced system of care achievable and applicable to modern Ireland. The idea is not to replace *in toto* our current system. After all, we will continue to need professional care and specialised health services. These cannot be simply done away with. Rather, the suggestion is to augment formal care by creating a network of basic structures and spaces to provide a minimum resource for people who require care. These basic structures of dialogic care may then form the nucleus for a radically reformed service. In this context, I will utilise the language of performance and metrics in order only to demonstrate systemic viability and to offer the possibility of a rapid transition. These proposals for a new system are a response to the urgency of the task before us.

The next chapter will critically assess the impact of neoliberal care, not just on how care systems are presently operating but also on how subjectivity is shaped by neoliberal modalities. This subjectivity serves as a barrier to seeking care because human need is today too often interpreted as a sign of personal failure rather than an issue of collective solidarity. We need to investigate just how profound our current challenges are in a technologically enhanced neoliberalism fundamentally inimical to a culture of care. It is in response to this that dialogic practice will be offered as an antidote. As outlined above, dialogue resituates care as a mutual relational task among people. Crucially, dialogue privileges the space *between* people as the location of focus, rather than modelling care as a transfer exchange of knowledge or resource from a knowing subject to a receiving object. Instead, dialogue requires the meeting of two subjectivities, together seeking to understand, define and address challenges. Dialogue requires time but it also requires a recognition that the outcomes of care relationships are not solely pre-determined by 'experts' but must be co-produced by subjects working together. The question of who precisely determines the metrics of success is critical in terms of locating power. Any new system must address quite specifically this question.

Following this conceptual clearing, Towards a Reformed Care System seeks to take up the challenge to outline viable care alternatives. Accordingly, I will explore in some detail *The Hologram* structure proposed by Cassie Thornton. This model grew out of her experience of *ad hoc* emergency care systems which developed in Greece during their recent economic collapse. As such, *The Hologram* is a minimum resource model, designed to function in situations of an almost complete loss of a formal care service. Could *The Hologram* model be both scaled up and, simultaneously, scaled down? Could it offer a dialogic model that could point the way to an alternative care system capable of application in Ireland? I want to investigate that possibility but without placing too great a burden on *The Hologram* experiment. However, it is dynamic and flexible, is an instantiation of a dialogical model, and carries within it what I regard as values and an architecture of care that has significant potential.

To achieve a culture of deep care we need almost a metaphysical reconstruction. This involves rescuing the neoliberal techno-subject out of their ideological entrancement and back into the messy relational dynamics of care reciprocity. The scale of this task is shown by trying to recover what are now counter-cultural words such as sacrifice, limit and self-denial as necessary properties of care practice. The final chapter therefore returns to the challenge posed to the sovereign subject by the materiality of care and seeks to resource the 'actually existing' caring commoner who either engages in or wishes to engage in care labour as an integral part of their humanity. This chapter examines the transforming potential of a universal basic income to animate and vitalise social connections and thus bring into the realm of the possible the enormous capacity inherent in a re-activated caring commons.

Care is a complex concept to define. It is so interwoven into our humanity that it is, as I noted above, rather challenging to confine it to a certain set of experiences or to demarcate it to a specific professional practice. Can it be distinguished from a host of intertwined human practices such as love, protection, nurturing?

Is care an emotion? Are you born with a caring disposition, or can it be learned almost as a skill? Why is it so difficult for some people to ask for care and then to receive it? Is becoming dependent on others not one of our great contemporary nightmares? Do we not think of being in receipt of care as rendering us a burden?

Margaret Mead famously identified the beginning of human civilisation with the discovery of an ancient healed human thighbone. The fact that it healed indicated that someone had stayed with the victim, keeping them alive until they were fit to move independently again. In other words, this instance of care signalled the move from animal solitary survival to human social care.

I am not intending here to survey the academic literature on care. I am more focused in this book on describing a new care model for application in Ireland. However, it may be helpful for our purposes to note Tronto's important explication of care in her 1993 book *Moral Boundaries: A political argument for an ethic of care*. There she outlined a definition of care as:

> On the most general level, we suggest that caring be viewed as a species activity that includes everything that we do to maintain, continue, and repair our 'world' so that we can live in it as well as possible. That world includes our bodies, our selves, and our environment, all of which we seek to interweave in a complex, life-sustaining web.[19]

This is quite a rich and inclusive formulation. She goes on to outline four phases of care. These are 'caring about' – 'the recognition in the first place that care is necessary';[20] 'taking care of' – 'assuming some responsibility for the identified need and determining how to respond to it';[21] 'care-giving' – which 'involves the direct meeting of needs for care';[22] and finally 'care-receiving' – which 'recognizes that the object of care will respond to the care it receives'.[23]

Tronto has refined this definition in later work but her distinctions remain heuristically valuable, especially in the task of assessing the effectiveness of formal systems of care. It remains true that many care needs are not recognised, and so the realm of what we 'care about' is constrained. These may include (as we will explore) the need to be heard and to have a voice in one's own care regime.

Tronto's definition has often been the starting point for considering the meaning of care in more recent academic work. Among the responses to her formulation has been a post-materialist perspective which has sought to recognise the importance of other non-human subjectivities. One interesting text in this regard is *Matters of Care: Speculative ethics in more than human worlds* by María Puig de la Bellacasa in which she offers this restatement of Tronto's proposal:

> We need an even more radically displaced non-humanist rephrasing of Joan Tronto and Berenice Fisher's generic notion of caring than I already proposed above by expanding 'our' world. We need to disrupt the subjective-collective behind the 'we': care is everything that is done (rather than everything that 'we' do) to maintain, continue, and repair 'the world' so that all (rather than 'we') can live in it as well as possible. That world includes ... all that we seek to inter-weave in a complex, life-sustaining web (modified from Tronto 1993, 103). What the 'all' includes in situation remains contingent to specific ecologies and human–nonhuman entanglements. What counts

is the 'interweaving' of living things that holds together worlds as we know them, that allows their perpetuation and renewal – and even that which helps to their decay as we have seen with the example of worms' labor of composting. Acknowledging the necessity of care in more than human relations, not as all that there is in a relation, not as a universal connection, but as something that traverses, that is passed on through entities and agencies, intensifies awareness of how beings depend on each other.[24]

The Care Manifesto: The politics of interdependence in 2020, presented by a number of authors under the designation 'The Care Collective', also sought to modify Tronto, this time from a more conventionally leftist position. The text suggests that Tronto's distinctions 'do not do justice to all care capacities and practices in their many diverse configurations and manifestations. Nor do they account for the paradoxes, ambivalences, and contradictions inherent in care and caretaking'.[25] Instead, it proposes a concept of universal care:

Universal care means we are all jointly responsible for hands-on care work, as well as engaging with and caring about the flourishing of other people and the planet. It means reclaiming forms of genuinely collective and communal life, adopting alternatives to capitalist markets, and reversing the marketisation of care infrastructures. It also means restoring and radically deepening our welfare states, both centrally and locally. And, finally, it means creating Green New Deals at the transnational level, caring international institutions and more porous borders, and cultivating everyday cosmopolitanism.

In *Compassionate Activism* I defined social care in specifically humanistic terms:

> … the core objective of what it is to care for someone is to be concerned with their liberation, by which is meant their personal and social transformation so that they can be who they truly are as persons and exercise a maximum of freedom and autonomy. The very essence of care is to liberate the person from all that binds them, from all that oppresses them and from all that curtails their freedom to be truly themselves. Thus care is a developmental, liberating endeavour. It seeks out the freedom of the other. It is about letting the other be fully human, liberated from the psychological and sociological oppressions that limit their humanity. In short, then, to care for someone is about participating in their integral liberation – personal and social – so that they can become fully human.[26]

The point here is to posit care as not about maintaining someone in a dependent state but to attend to their maximum self-realisation as a person and to act to remove all those barriers to that. This has echoes of the deep-ecologist philosopher Arne Naess' claim that full self-realisation of all beings is the ontological principle for an ecological world.[27] Crucially though, the autonomy and realisation prioritised here is not into separation but connection.

At a minimum level of understanding though, and to offer an orientation for the task undertaken in this text, I want to propose that the work of care be centred on the quality of our *response* to the needs and vulnerability of an other. That other may be human or other-than-human. In short, the quality of our care is calibrated with the quality of our response to the needs of the other. My focus here is on the *practice* of care rather than on an overly philosophical exploration. As I have indicated above, I want to explore this practice within two overlapping dimensions – that of professional social care and that situated within the commons of human exchange, relationships and conviviality. While I will keep each dimension in view throughout, I will treat each in turn given the differences between them. The intention is to offer a re-imagining of care which, though necessarily limited in detail, offers a clear direction of travel towards a reform of the care system but, more ambitiously, a re-orientation to care which returns us to the actual empirical sources of human support found in the caring commons.

The Dialogic Solution

I n the last chapter I argued that our problem of care provision results from the impact of two forces. On the one hand, we are producing an ever-greater need for care while at the same time our systems of care are unable to adequately respond because of lack of capacity. The result is a growing deficit which is manifested in waiting lists, poor-quality treatment and support, growing frustration and stress for care workers and care receivers, and increased and often unnecessary human suffering. Once again, it should be emphasised that this is not a consequence of personal failure. The problem is systemic.

A story may illustrate. Many years ago, I was a participant in an informal care initiative called *Trialogue*.[28] It involved regular public meetings and discussions open to anyone interested in the topic of mental health and wellness. This could include those with lived experience, professionals working in the field, or members of the community – hence the term trialogue. Topics would be agreed in advance or decided at the gathering.

I recall at one meeting an elderly man who was a regular attender speaking very animatedly about a radio discussion he had just heard about mental ill-health. At the end of the discussion the presenter said that the most important thing to remember for those listening was to ensure that they spoke to someone about their mental health challenges. The man exclaimed with exasperation, 'Who do I speak to? And what do I say to them?'

I felt at the time, and do so even more now, that these were profound questions. For many people the primary issue is who can they in fact speak to about their issues and challenges. Even if you successfully identify such a person, what exactly do you say to them? What is the language of emotion, of feeling, of distress, and how do you use it in such a way that that person can appropriately respond to you? Where are the places where any of this can actually be done?

In many ways, this short book is an attempt to address the two questions posed by that man. For this reason, my focus is on exploring the outlines of a possible solution, applicable to present-day Ireland. Nonetheless, before doing so, I need to at least sketch out the primary features of the problem we are trying to address. To do this, we need an overview of the neoliberal landscape. I do not propose to define or analyse neoliberalism in any detail or enter the debate on whether our system is adequately characterised as 'neoliberal'. This task has been accomplished elsewhere. For example, the reader can be usefully directed to a previous text in this *Síreacht* series – Eilís Ward's book *Self* (2021). Kathleen Lynch has also completed a book on this which touches on some of the themes that I am addressing – *Care and Capitalism: Why affective equality matters for social justice* (2022). My concern is specifically on the effect of neoliberalism as an operational set of assumptions and practices on our system of care and on our wider culture. I will briefly examine this impact in three distinct dimensions. First, how neoliberalism creates new care needs; secondly, how neoliberalism curtails and calibrates how social care systems respond; and finally, how neoliberalism impacts on our caring subjectivities.

After this short overview, I want then to take the first step into the imagined realm of an alternative model. This model begins with an invitation to a form of paradigm shift where a new meta-metric is proposed which re-orders the operational modality of the care system from one of service coverage to one of dialogue. Dialogue recovers care as a *relationship* between two subjects who meet in a mutual exchange, in contrast to exchanges that are in effect commodity transactions, where a subject confers a service on an object. Restoring relationships to the centre of care allows us to orient care (even professional social care) back towards the commons, where non-commodified relationships are the very essence of human sociality and well-being.

At first glance though this can seem a somewhat tame shift and certainly not particularly revolutionary in the Kuhnian sense. However, what is important to recognise is that the logic of neoliberal care culminates in an array of performance indicator metrics, overseen by a managerial cadre. The attainment of these pre-determined indicators purports to offer a simulacrum of 'market discipline' by judging the competitive success of care providers (indeed even individual care workers within organisations) with the achievement of these indicators. Can we imagine a care system where, if we must have them, the metrics of care are set by care receivers themselves? A dialogic care practice invites users of services, in dialogue with professionals, to themselves determine the intended outcome of the care. The revolutionary potential in this shift is glimpsed when one imagines the hitherto impossible scenario whereby a service user may decide that owning a house, having efficient transport, having adequate heat are in fact the care outcomes they want rather than merely a new wheelchair, a place on a training programme or medication. Dialogue as a meta-metric mandating how the care system is actually delivered offers at least the possibility of freeing the neoliberal subject to construct new and potentially subversive outcome targets. It is a form of social aikido – using the very impetus of neoliberal procedures (in this case outcome metrics) to produce the very opposite of what is offered within a capitalist imaginary.

Systems of care reflect the wider social structure of which they are necessarily a part. Thus, the incarceration/ confinement models of the nineteenth century drew on the social assumptions of the time regarding hygiene as an ordering principle for modern social space. In the same way that sewage and wastewater should be piped away from public visibility, so too were unwanted humans removed from social interaction. Similarly, today's social care is shaped by today's dominant rationality and becomes an instrument of that rationality. Rather than becoming a node of contestation, it becomes instead a mechanism of reproduction. Thus, the efficacy of much current social care is judged by how successfully service users might be better integrated into the labour market. Employment and employability become indicators of 'success'. Helping people make the 'right choices' becomes in practice a methodology for market integration. The life-coach emerges as a new agent of care, a role designed to encourage people to adopt the appropriate set of attitudes and motivations, combined with the requisite skills, for entry into the 'competitive' jobs marketplace.

Understanding the framing impact of our dominant social theory is crucial if we are in turn to understand the way in which human beings' natural orientation to care – natural in the sense of being a key adaptation constitutive of our humanity as social beings – nonetheless gets shaped and conditioned by the social world. The individual expression of care – using all four of Tronto's modes – becomes articulated within the available categories of the social structure.

Neoliberalism and care

As I noted above, I want to outline our dominant system's impact on care by examining it in three dimensions. First, in terms of the demand for care, neoliberalism has profoundly influenced what needs are being generated. Several specific aspects can be noted in this regard.

At its most obvious and perhaps harshest, neoliberalism has reduced the reach and depth of the social welfare state. The high point of social welfare support in the West was in the immediate post-Second World War decades, but following the Thatcher–Reagan political axis from 1980 onwards the welfare state became politically problematised. Welfare-receipt was rendered a dubious status. References to the 'citizen' as the primary subject of liberal democracy gave way to the category of the 'tax-payer', by which was really meant a paid employee. The return to nineteenth-century standards of social utility as based on labour relegated large numbers of people from value and support. Ireland largely embraced these political ideas. Here, there was not so much a contraction of welfare services as a growing difficulty in meeting qualifying criteria and restrictive income thresholds.[29]

In addition, the withdrawal of the state from public utility provision in favour of private providers reflected the belief in the commodification of services and their necessary improvement within a free-market competitive construct. Waste-disposal services were removed from local authorities and handed over to private companies who charged customers for waste removal. The traditional public utilities such as telephones, electricity, bus transport were *de facto* privatised. Even road construction gave way to various public–private initiatives, with tolling a feature of the modern Irish motorway. The current housing disaster is in part the result of the withdrawal of the state from the construction of affordable social housing.[30] Increasingly, citizens in receipt of services were replaced as a conceptual category by customers choosing to purchase products.

The emptying of institutions of care from the 1960s onwards reflected changes in care philosophy but also suited the narrative of state disinvestment in welfare and its supposed role in creating welfare dependency. The loss of institutions was of strangely mixed benefit because the required community-based infrastructure to support newly de-institutionalised people was often limited.[31]

The 'reforming' of social welfare and social spending made people more vulnerable to an inherent feature of the capitalist economy, namely the production of social inequality. The 2022 Survey on Income and Living Conditions from the CSO shows that 13.1 per cent of the population was at risk of poverty, up from 11.6 per cent in 2021.[32] 5.3 per cent were living in consistent poverty, a significant increase on the 4 per cent figure in 2021. Some 691,587 people were experiencing deprivation, of whom 204,710 were children. These figures are of significance because we know that the single greatest indicator of social problems – and therefore of social care needs – is inequality. In simple terms, the more inequality, the more social problems (other factors being equal). Despite some contestation, this clear causal link is supported by numerous and varied studies.[33] What this means is that inequality produces the need for care. It is therefore predictable that of the 200,000-plus children in Ireland experiencing deprivation today, a significant proportion of those will require social care services as adults in the future.

This issue of inequality is a large and complex one. I am glossing over it quickly as my focus is on how a modern care system for Ireland might better respond to these escalating care needs. Suffice it to say that the competitive, atomised market model of neoliberalism inevitably creates winners and losers. The losers require care to function as their reduced resources and social status imposes stresses and strains that become manifest in a multiple of material ways such as poor housing, inadequate heating, limited food quality, which in turn leads to ever-worsening relative physical and mental health needs. All of this requires greater social and health care responses and growing demands for ever more care resourcing. Yet this response can never be enough in a political atmosphere of minimising personal taxation and balancing budgets, so that inevitable further casualties result. Those who need care do not receive it in a sufficient manner. Given the ideological hegemony in play, there is little or no political demand for focusing politics away from arguments over the size of the buckets needed to capture the flow of care needs towards instead addressing the tap of inequality producing them in the first place. Reducing inequality is an unpopular political project in today's Ireland. This is one reason why giving service users control of the metrics of care performance would be so subversive. They are, as suggested above, highly likely to pay attention to addressing causes, not symptoms.

A feature that I will note further below is that our neoliberal world also produces greater isolation for individuals. The loss of the structures of social connection accentuates growing trends towards loneliness, which is a critical factor in mental and physical ill-health.[34] According to the CSO, almost a quarter of Irish households in 2016 (397,510) were single-person occupied.[35] This is a matter that I will return to in The Commons of Care because it is not enough to have a better-designed care *system* – we need to address the root causes giving rise to care needs in the first place, among which is the erosion of the social and caring commons. Provision of a universal basic income would provide both immediate resources and the capacity to build new networks of connection.

It should furthermore be recognised that, as we survey the twenty-first century, new and additional care needs can be anticipated. This will particularly arise from the ongoing and increasing effects of climate breakdown. While the exact nature of these needs remains uncertain in a specifically Irish context, we can anticipate the loss of homes due to flooding and erosion, the loss of livelihoods through economic instability, and the yet unpredictable but emerging phenomenon of climate-related depression and despair. The social care of the future may be centred on emergency accommodation, food growing, local energy production and maintaining elementary social services at a community level.

The second dimension of the neoliberal impact on formal care is its profound effect on how care services are delivered and structured. A very useful and insightful analysis of this was conducted by John Harris in his book *The Social Work Business*. There Harris shows how the pressure of neoliberal ideology and resultant practices has transformed social work and social care by altering their operating principles from those based on public service welfare provision to those derived instead from private-sector free-market businesses. This switch in conceptual field from care as public service to care as private business has greatly contributed to the resource-constrained and performance-driven corporate care model we see today. It is not that good care work does not still get done. It is rather that this is accomplished in the teeth of the prevailing headwinds of corporate compliance metrics which prioritise outcomes and target-attainment rather than the temporally open, unfolding relationship of optimum care. Actualised care appears constantly in a rush, with something else always needing to be done, and accompanying paperwork to be completed. The impetus driving this transformation is not confined to the impact of privatisation. The state's introduction of regulation and professionalisation in social care has also directed care work towards 'evidence-based' performatives. Harris' book describes this process in detail in the UK, but Ireland too is undergoing similar regulated professionalisation of social care overseen by the state body CORU. As in the UK, the objective of the process is to produce a professional social care workforce whose qualification criteria are achieved through demonstrable standards of proficiency which can be measured and assessed in *de facto* training programmes delivered by third level colleges. As Mulkeen concludes in her study of care in the context of the CORU standards of proficiency:

> In its relative neglect of the relational dimension of care and the more serious neglect of the emotional labour of care, the standards reveal a highly technical -rational approach to care. In addition, there is little of the language of care; interdependence, solidarity, loyalty, reciprocity, altruism, friendship, and love in the standards or how these can be developed as components of professional practice.[36]

As we know, ideology functions when it is the unspoken, taken-for-granted background of everyday practice. That care should be more like a corporate service, and care workers more like a target-led, supervised workforce, is simply now a given. In a later more succinct outline of the impact of neoliberalism, Harris identifies three distinct aspects of its refashioning of social work which apply equally to social care and related care services. These are marketisation, consumerisation and managerialisation. They are each derived from core elements of neoliberal thought. As Harris summarises:

> Markets are efficient and effective and should be introduced in as many and as wide a range of contexts as possible. Individuals should be responsible for themselves and run their own lives. Services in the public or voluntary sectors should be modelled on management knowledge and techniques drawn from the private business sector.[37]

The application of these processes to social care provision has redefined the relationship between care givers and receivers. This is now structured as more akin to customers choosing a care commodity from a suite of competing providers. Perhaps the greatest impact, though, has been the emergence of a management apparatus designed to 'manage' care by employing approaches and strategies first developed for business practices.

The impact of neoliberal managerialism on social work can be found in three key trends:

- Commodification involves identifying discrete problem categories and a menu of service options in order to quantify and cost service outputs. This often reduces social work to a series of one-off transactions, depriving it of meaningful working relationships with and commitments to service users.

- Reducing funding to produce efficiency gains exerts downward pressure on costs by imitating the pressure towards falling profits in capitalist markets.

- Exerting greater control over professional space, for example through the use of 'dashboards' as a means of heightening surveillance of the work of individual social workers and groups of social workers.[38]

Paul Verhaeghe's 2014 book *What About Me? The struggle for identity in a market-based society* provides an analysis, from a psychological perspective, of the effect of these processes on care practice. In the newly remodelled 'care business', variations of 'rank and yank'[39] performance indicators, in which certain metrics of achievement are incentivised, result in workers only doing what literally counts. If it does not count, why do it? In this way, much that might be regarded as 'caring' labour becomes first invisible (it is simply not counted) and then abandoned by overwhelmed workers as having no outward value or utility. As Verhaeghe observes: 'Wherever quantitative yardsticks are used to measure quality, behaviour soon adapts to the system, invariably leading to a loss of diversity.'[40] He cites a doctor, Marc Desmet, who set out four management symptoms experienced in his work. The first entails non-stop changes in the working environment – new software, new corporate structures. The second is the 'Big Brother' feeling of constant evaluation, review and audits. The changes themselves are rarely subject to such analysis, rather it is nearly always the staff. The third symptom is how more and more of one's time is focused on administration, management and monitoring rather than the work itself.

Finally, there's the symptom that Desmet calls 'dispiriting contradictions'. Everyone is constantly urged to cut costs, yet they see vast amounts being spent on items that serve no real purpose. Like hiring a consultancy to devise a new name and slogan that should, above all, not be taken literally ('We're here for you!'), or ordering accounting software that's considered useless by those in the know and ends up costing twice as much as predicted. Another creeping symptom is bombastic use of language. Besides ugly terms such as 'service users' for patients and 'disinvestment' for cuts, health-sector documents are bursting at the seams with claims to excellence. An individual who blew his or her own trumpet so loudly would risk being diagnosed with narcissistic personality disorder.[41]

One can readily see how dispiriting indeed this work environment would be. Nonetheless, the care worker can quickly be acclimatised into a mode of practice adapted to this setting. If not, they simply become exhausted, burnt-out, and ultimately leave. As is well acknowledged, the so-called burnout level in frontline care work is very high.[42]

The result is that we have carers who themselves are not well cared for. If the metrics by which their work is measured focus on issues other than the quality of care for themselves and care receivers, then the inherent stress of care work is greatly accentuated. This is quite a significant issue and one that the proposal I outline in Towards a Reformed Care System seeks to address.

Finally, the third dimension of neoliberalism's impact on care lies in how it shapes the human subject to both be more fragile and vulnerable and, at the same time, paradoxically less likely to seek care. The key to understanding this apparent dilemma is to recognise the ideological construct of the self-interested rational actor who is imagined to be the self-choosing author of their own life. If everything is up to me, then there are no social problems. There are only bad personal choices. If I need care, it can only be because I have made poor choices. This makes me a meritocratically determined 'loser'. My subsequent need for care makes socially visible the shame of my personal inadequacy. Yet, it is my very isolation which renders me far more vulnerable to life's challenges than were I socially connected with access to wider resources.

In a way, this extreme attention on the individual as creator of reality is the logical culmination of humanist liberalism. If the individual is the author of their own life, and there are no limits to self-actualisation other than those that are self-imposed, then the burden of achieving happiness and well-being falls inevitably on oneself. As Renata Salecl has observed:

In Western capitalist society everything in people's lives appears to be a matter of choice. One can choose one's identity, sexual orientation, religion, to have or not have children. One is free to remodel one's body, even change gender, and one hopes to have some power over the ultimate incurable in one's life – when and how to die. Foucault's vision from his last works on the history of sexuality was to make out of ourselves a work of art. Today it appears as though this proposition has been fully embraced by the dominant ideology.[43]

In her book *The Tyranny of Choice* she outlines how the modern western subject has no choice but to choose. If everything is one's own choice, then one is responsible for everything. 'When individuals are made to feel they are the masters of their own destiny, and when positive thinking is offered as the panacea for the ills that they suffer as the result of social injustice, social critique is increasingly replaced by self-critique.'[44] The consequence is today's observable focus on well-being, self-improvement, physical fitness. Care is directed inwards on oneself because the unhappy self is the centre of personal anxiety. Self-care is regarded as an obligation for each individual and indeed almost a mandatory component of one's working and personal life. As Eilís Ward pointed out in *Self*, this leads to an absorption, diverting the gaze from the outer world to the inner one of personal feeling, emotion and mind, producing a 'therapy culture'. Salecl concludes:

> The feeling of shame for being poor and of guilt for not getting further up the ladder of economic success has replaced the fight against social injustice. And the anxiety about not being good enough has pacified people, leading them not only to work longer hours but often to work just as hard at their appearance. Choice can open up the possibility of change at the level of society, but only when it is no longer perceived as solely an individual prerogative. The success of the ideology of choice in today's society has been in blinding people to the fact that their actual choices are becoming severely limited by the social divisions in society and that issues such as the organisation of labour, health and safety, and the environment appear more and more beyond their choice. At the level of society we are therefore losing the possibility of choice in terms of change in power relations as we

know them. Not surprisingly, the ideology of choice goes hand and hand with the New Age ideology that promotes living in the moment and accepting things as they are.[45]

What in large part drives all of this is the superego imperative to be happy. Happiness is presented as the goal of a healthy and fulfilled life. Anything which prevents my personal happiness is now designated as the new iniquity which must be removed, aided by the 'high priests' of personal well-being such as mentors, influencers, motivational speakers and gurus, life coaches, popular psychologists.[46] Desire – unleashed to the maximum in contemporary capitalism – is the guiding star to happiness. Desire must be indulged. Indeed, not to do so is defined as a symptom of repression. If you put up with your bad teeth, overweight stomach, bad relationship, then it is your fault. You can do something about it and you ought to. There is nothing to stop you. The superego injunction is to aim for your personal dream and realise it.

When you combine this imperative with the possibilities offered by the internet then the personal project of desire maximisation becomes radically accentuated. The algorithms guiding the internet fix themselves around you and mirror your desire back to you. Your very preferences – your clicks, your likes, your searches – become data to build a wholly personalised internet experience where your every yearning, vulnerability, and preference becomes amplified and is fed back to you in a great circular loop luring you ever forward into your own desired universe.[47] You strive forward, with the carrot before your nose becoming ever more desirable.

Equality metamorphoses into becoming a claim to my right to pursue my happiness in my way. It is less about solidarity and sharing and more about allowing everyone to be happy in whatever way they wish. Hence, traditional transgression becomes remodelled as forms of personal expression and therefore beyond social criticism. Indeed, having one's individual choice questioned by another is now experienced as oppressive and judgemental.[48]

Jaron Lanier, one of the founders of artificial reality technology, has expressed grave concerns at this direction in human subjectivity. In his book *You Are Not a Gadget* he warns that the impact of information technology is to arrest human personal development: 'You have to be somebody before you can share yourself.'[49] 'The deep meaning of personhood is being reduced by illusions of bits.'[50]

The greatest impediment to this sanctification of individual choice is the notion of limits. The claim that there might be legitimate limits to choice must in principle be resisted because such a claim is too deeply at odds with the self-actualising pursuit of desire. Hence, moral limits are disparaged as outdated and primitive, and eco-limits are gestured towards but never observed.

It is in this precise way that neoliberal subjectivity is inimical to the labour of care. Care interrupts the desiring self in its project of personal realisation. It interdicts the claim to autonomy. This is simply because the materialisation of care – its organic, physical and temporal challenges – involves necessarily a sacrifice of self and of the self-referential project of the self. The demand of care – whether to another or indeed to my own self – requires a giving of my time and my labour. The care needs of another demand a response from me, a response that may divert me from my personal desires. In a neoliberal framework this diversion can only be experienced as a negative, an interruption. In his well-known article addressing the parents of autistic children, the autistic activist Jim Sinclair highlights the real pain and loss involved in recognising the reality of having a neurodivergent child:

> After you've started that letting go, come back and look at your autistic child again, and say to yourself: 'This is not my child that I expected and planned for. This is an alien child who landed in my life by accident. I don't know who this child is or what it will become. But I know it's a child, stranded in an alien world, without parents of its own kind to care for it. It needs someone to care for it, to teach it, to interpret and to advocate for it. And because this alien child happened to drop into my life, that job is mine if I want it.'[51]

The care demand of the other imposes an obligation. In truth, what I have wryly called 'really existing' human beings know this. This is how human beings actually function. Every parent, every care giver knows this. Yet the neoliberal conceit is put before us relentlessly so that those 'burdened' with care demands, those who are caught up in 'cares', are presented as living less fulfilled lives. This is because their personal desires are seen as compromised by the needs of others. Without a culture that affirms the work of care, no amount of structural reform in care systems will suffice.

Yet such reforms are nonetheless necessary. It is to that task that I wish now to turn. In Towards a Reformed Care System I will explore how we might practically redesign our care system to achieve better-quality care service. Before that, I want to elaborate on the potential of dialogic practice to orientate our direction of travel. The suggestion is that if we could design dialogue as a meta-metric of our care system we could fashion it in a new, more effective and more caring direction.

Dialogic practice

The test of efficacy to be applied is that a new configuring of our care system needs to be able to respond to each of the three aspects of the neoliberal challenge. We need to be able to reduce care needs (demand), improve care response (supply) and change the subjectivities being shaped by neoliberalism. It is to this challenge that dialogue is presented as an 'elegant' response – elegant in the sense of a seemingly small change producing a significant consequence. So, what do we mean by dialogue? What precisely is it and why might it hold the key to a radical transformation?[52]

One way to approach the meaning of dialogue is to consider its opposite – monologue. The Finnish psychologist and advocate of dialogic practice Jaakko Seikkula notes:

> Bräten (1988) described monologue as seeing the other as passive. Interpersonally, monologue involves silencing the other by domination or by control of the available means of explanation. Intrapsychically, monologue restricts one's internal representation of the other (Bräten's [1992] 'Virtual Other') to the position of echoing and ratifying the inner voice of the self.[53]

Much of our current care system is characterised by a 'speaking down' to the care receiver. The expert is the 'subject who knows' – the service user is the object who receives. Mikhail Bakhtin's judgement is particularly apt here: 'For the word (and, consequently, for a human being) there is nothing more terrible than a lack of response.'[54] Multiple studies show how devastating it is for human well-being to be ignored, not listened to or not replied to. Dialogue aims to completely change this dynamic.

At its most basic, dialogue involves two movements – that of *listening to* and *responding to* the words and experiences of the other person. It is grounded in the objective of giving people the power to define and solve their own problems as uncovered in the very process of dialogue itself. The dialogic care process includes the person, their family and supporters, and relevant professionals. In this approach, attention is on the space between people. That is where problems are located. They are not the property of one person – the one who presents with the issue or challenge – but rather occur when this issue or challenge is not responded to appropriately. Only then do we have a problem which is in fact shared by both sides because it is made up of both the challenge and the quality of response to that challenge.

The caring power of this double movement of call–response lies in its deep anthropological and biological roots. The work of the child psychologist Colwyn Trevarthen shows how the new-born infant almost immediately engages in dialogical exchanges with their parents or primary care givers by utilising facial expressions, hand movements and modulated vocalisations.[55] The infant is seeking to influence its care givers and cause a response in them, and the quality of that adult response in turn profoundly impacts on the emotional state and well-being of the child. The nature of the adult response literally shapes the structure of the developing brain. This has enormous implications for that child and for how we might in turn elaborate a renewed culture of care. Thus, the primal roots of the dialogic movement of sound/gesture and listening lies in the infant cry and adult response. The soothing presence of the emotionally attuned adult is of utmost importance and offers us the very foundational experience of care.

There are many ways to describe a professional dialogical practice. I will outline one such practice in terms of assumptions, principles, method and implications. It should be noted that there are many dialogical variations and methodologies. I am selecting one only to illustrate a practical application. Once again, my concern is with addressing a meta-metric possibility in order to re-imagine social care in modern Ireland. Crucially, dialogic care requires time, acceptance, genuine communication and a willingness on the part of the carer to encounter the person they are working with on the plain of their common humanity. But the test of the value of this approach is effectiveness. Not only can it be shown to work but I think it can be further demonstrated that a dialogic process in itself restores humanity to both care receiver and care giver. It does so by recognising that human beings are not objects. Their behaviour is not always predictable. They are not units within a Newtonian universe who respond equally to the application of similar 'forces' or 'inputs'. They do not always clearly and immediately understand the motivations, traumas or underlying causes for their own conduct. Today's dominant managerialist approach to care assumes the homogeneity and predictability of people who require similar sets of 'incentives' in order to do the 'right' things. If they do not, then the temptation in this context is to blame service users for being 'difficult' and 'unresponsive' and, as a result, to further reinforce modes of oppressive practice. However, often the failures that we are experiencing lie not with the people we work with but with the inappropriate non-dialogic (even anti-dialogic) methods we are following.

The many classical theorists of dialogue (from Socrates onwards) have in common the recognition that human well-being and the search for meaning involve subjects in communicative interaction with others. As I have noted above, dialogic theories suggest that understanding and sense is to be found *between* subjects rather than being contained *within* the solitary subject or imagined as involving a transfer of knowledge from one to another. For example, for Martin Buber, human inter-subjectivity comes prior to individualisation. In his well-known terminology, the relations I–Thou or I–It precede the I itself. Openness and attentiveness to 'meeting' the other allow us to relate to the other as to a *Thou*; being enclosed within our experiences and uses of the other leads us to relate to the other as to an *It*. Buber proposes that our very personhood is determined by the manner of our relations with others: 'A person makes his appearance by entering into relation with other persons.'[56]

For Bakhtin it is the response to the word of the other that is at the heart of what is involved in dialogue. Dialogue is far more than technique – it touches on the essence of being human and of humanisation: '[A]uthentic human life is the open-ended dialogue. Life by its very nature is dialogic. To live means to participate in dialogue.'[57]

In the next chapter I will briefly mention a system of mental health care developed in northern Finland called Open Dialogue. This approach rests on bringing people with mental health challenges into early dialogue with therapists and family members. A central theorist of this approach is Jaakko Seikkula. His book, co-written with Tom Erik Arnkill, *Dialogical Meetings in Social Networks*, elaborates a theory and practice of dialogue. This is developed by him in further writings:

> For as I see it, dialogue is not a method; it is a way of life. We learn it as one of the first things in our lives, which explains why dialogue can be such a powerful happening. Because it is the basic ruling factor of life, it is in fact very simple. It is its very simplicity that seems to be the paradoxical difficulty. It is so simple that we cannot believe that the healing element of any practice is simply to be heard, to have response, and that when the response is given and received, our therapeutic work is fulfilled. Our clients have regained agency in their lives by having the capacity for dialogue.[58]

In a similar vein, Paulo Freire placed the contrast between dialogics and antidialogics as central to his theory of education. Dialogue for him is the key instrument of human liberation by which human beings discover and name the world and imagine how that world might be reconstructed.

> Antidialogue is an instrument of oppression by which human beings are instructed by those who claim to know and whose voice is thereby silenced. Thus, antidialogue (or monologue – one person speaks and the other listens) reduces human beings 'to the status of things'.[59]

> Dialogue is the encounter between men, mediated by the world, in order to name the world ... If it is in speaking their word that men transform the world by naming it, dialogue imposes itself as the way in which men achieve significance as men. Dialogue is thus an existential necessity.[60]

How does all of this translate into a reformed approach to care? My proposal is that re-orienting our care system towards a dialogic approach re-positions it to respond far better to human care needs, has a better long-term impact on reducing care needs in the first place, and restores human mutuality and social connection. In the next chapter I will outline a practical model for application to the formal care system drawn from *The Hologram* proposal of Cassie Thornton, which allows dialogue to become the mode of care praxis.

The fundamental approach in a dialogic care system is to take the challenges that people have and turn them into questions and use these questions to generate dialogue between care receivers, their supporters/family and professional carers. Thus, challenges become questions, questions become dialogue. Questions, properly framed and authentically addressed, give us the orientation we require to locate answers. Crucially, these questions are set by the care receivers. Their resolution to the satisfaction of care receivers in turn becomes the 'metric' by which care outcomes are assessed. In short, if intended outcomes are not co-produced dialogically, then they are not appropriate or humanly valid. In this way, the performance-driven, results-based indicators of our managerialist system become reconfigured by a switch in how the metrics of 'success' are determined. Dialogue becomes a method which creates co-produced metrics – as I have suggested above, a new meta-metric. In this way, the care system becomes programmed to respond to genuine needs as determined by care-receiving individuals, rather than a system offering a pre-determined menu of discrete services. We can speculate that preferred outcomes for care receivers may well therefore extend beyond the conventional care responses and enter into wider socio-political needs such as poverty, housing, food, heating, and so on. The care system then, to meet its new metrics, would be obliged to engage in the securing of these issues. The radical nature of this, how novel this may strike us, is an indicator of the constraints of the contemporary care reach and points to why we have ever-increasing care needs and an inadequate care response.

A dialogic practice such as I am proposing here can be described in a number of steps. These include its purpose, its underlying principles, its goals, its core assumption and its working methodology. To make this clearer, and avoid any charge of abstraction, let me present the summary below.

Purpose
Giving people the power to define and solve their own problems.

Principles
The process is as important as the outcome.
People can be trusted to make the right decision.
Democracy should characterise care practice.
Dialogue is a mode of discovery of self and the world.

Goals
Goals must be clear.
Humanisation is an ultimate goal.
Goals are to be set by subjects themselves in dialogue and are outlined in a 'specific generating question' which emerges in the dialogue – e.g. What is it that we need in order to … ?

Core assumption
Those affected by issues are the best sources of knowledge about what needs to be done.

Working methodology
Develop in dialogue a generating question around a

defined problematic.

Facilitate the person or group to generate answers.

Provide/source the tools and resources to permit the person or group to implement their answers.

The person or group is accountable.

Learn, reflect and re-do.

Dialogic practice needs

Time.

Non-judgemental acceptance.

Real communication – genuine listening and authentic response.

The meeting place of our common humanity.

Implications for professional practice

Social care practitioners become facilitators of the humanisation process.

An orientation around service response rather than service coverage.

Central skill becomes relationship-formation and the capacity and willingness to enter into dialogue.

Outcomes are determined by the receivers of care services.

Each of these steps warrants being elaborated in detail, but that would be unnecessarily lengthy. For now, and for the purposes of creating a context for the further elaboration of a reformed Irish care system, I will confine myself to a few brief comments. Crucial, however, is to recognise that the fundamental purpose of such a dialogic process is to permit the individual or group to have the power to both define and resolve their own problems. This is the pivotal aspect by which the *system* supports the *commons*. Critical to this is the power of definition. The capacity to name and identify the problem at issue is a key expression of social power. It is here that the authority traditionally exercised by the professional becomes most apparent. A truly liberating practice acknowledges the right and capability of the care receiver to exercise control over definition. This is a key purpose in a dialogical process and allows the emergence of new metrics of success. Much error and indeed abuse has arisen in social care from imposing definitions of problems on people rather than engaging with them to achieve a shared understanding of what needs to be resolved.

The hopeful perspective opened up here is that people can in fact be trusted to make the right decision. In other words, given the right information, adequate resources and professional support, people will almost inevitably come up with the appropriate decisions. So much of our contemporary managerially based systems are built around an inherent distrust of 'clients', a facile assumption that without adequate restrictions or incentives they won't act in a positive manner. Hence, we have numerous social and institutional systems imposing models such as those described by George Ritzer in his 'McDonaldization' thesis. Indeed, a proper focus on a *process* that is liberating through meaningful dialogue almost always ensures that the *outcome* will take care of itself. Once more, managerialism's obsession with measurable performance indicators forces care workers to prioritise visible deliverables that often are of minimal or transient benefit to care receivers (e.g. the quantity of meetings held rather than the qualitative consequence of those meetings). Instead of pre-set outcomes into which each individual must fit irrespective of their individual circumstances, dialogic practice permits us to be open to the as yet unknown answer that can only be uncovered in the process of dialogue. We need therefore to be willing to work within this initial unknow-ingness, what Seikkula designates as a 'tolerance of uncertainty'.

However, this unknowingness is not directionless. What the specific goals are and how those goals are to be achieved requires elaboration. But this is itself the outcome of dialogue. The challenges faced by people should be turned into generating questions, i.e. questions designed to generate solutions. In one year's time, how would I like my life to be? How shall I find purpose and socially meaningful work? How will we address the issue of young people's lack of facilities in our community? These questions emerge in the dialogue following a grappling with understanding and defining problems. The questions can then be used to launch the search for answers in further dialogic unravelling involving professionals, clients and their supporters. The ultimate goal, within which all other goals are contained, is the humanisation and social recognition of the participants. This humanisation process and ethic underscores the more practical processes underway so that, even if immediate goals are not realised or are partially realised, the participants are not reduced in their basic humanity. The dialogue itself has been a progressive experience, one that creates commons-oriented resources, capacities and resilience that can serve into the future. Thus, dialogue begins to erode the need for formal care responses at all.

The fundamental assumption framing this entire method is that those affected by issues are the best sources of knowledge about what needs to be done. This includes not just those with an identifiable care issue but those also more widely affected by that problem – family, friends, community. I do not say that they are the *only* source of knowledge, but they are the best source. This is because it is they who live within the holistic existential reality of the issue and have therefore access to far greater data and understanding than anyone outside of this reality. In this way, our model of expertise may need to be refined. The professional is not someone who necessarily 'knows' but rather one who must learn. The expert is the person who is most affected by an issue and is thus the one who must disclose the meanings of what is happening. By listening and responding, the professional comes to gain insight and knowledge not available to them prior to a dialogic engagement. To suggest that it is, is to claim superiority over the meaning and words of the other.

A specific working methodology for the professional carer, somewhat mirroring Freire's see-judge-act approach, can be set out as follows. First is to enter into the process of dialogue with those affected by the issue. In this process the issue is explored and defined and from this a generating question is developed. Second, the resultant dialogue is orientated towards finding answers or solutions. Third, solutions need to be implemented as best as is possible. This requires the mobilisation of resources and knowledge. It is here that the professional's role becomes important. However, the application of resources from the professional to the client has occurred following a dialogic inductive process rather than from an 'expertly' framed deductive intervention. Fourth, it is of utmost importance that if those affected by the issue define their question and determine its solution, then they are accountable. Taking responsibility for implementing actions and plans is part of the humanisation and social recognition of the person. Finally, care givers and receivers must engage continually in a critical reflection on their practice. Primarily, we need this reflection because mistakes are inevitable. They are part of life, part of being human. No methodology is infallible, not least because we are dealing with human beings, who do not behave in a predictable manner. The way to address mistakes is to learn from them.

In order for this dialogic practice to best perform, more than just will is required. One key resource needed is time. As we noted above, in contemporary organisations time is carefully rationed and controlled. Yet, meaningful dialogue requires time because talking needs trust, security and the context of an authentic relationship. None of this can happen quickly. Time is needed to show non-judgemental acceptance of the other – to permit them to feel safe to express their unique word and thereby gain purchase on themselves and the world.

In outlining this approach, I do not at all wish to understate the challenge of constructing organisations designed around dialogic response rather than service coverage. It requires organisations that are genuinely flexible and smart rather than bureaucratic. It requires practitioners whose central skills become those of relationship-formation and the capacity to enter into meaningful dialogue rather than skills of prescription and direction. Care workers must become more democratic, more liberatory, more dialogic. Rather than professional 'fixers', they become facilitators of the humanisation process.

However, all of this may sound quite impractical or overly idealistic. There are objections that can be advanced on conceptual and practical grounds. Many care needs require immediate interventions, not drawn-out dialogic response. An overly extended dialogic encounter may simply delay much-needed action. But the argument here is simply that it is for the seeker of care to determine what their needs are. Where people are heard, responded to and socially acknowledged and connected, we inevitably have a superior system of care, one far better adapted to human reality than neoliberalism's managed, resource-deficient system. A dialogic meta-metric, co-produced by care receivers and care givers, legally mandated as a condition of care funding and delivery, offers a far greater prospect for delivering meaningful care.

In the model of neoliberal care such a change appears impossible. It is not compatible with the managed functionality of the current system. But is it possible at all? Can it
be shown to actually work? It cannot if our frame is care as
commodity. For it to work, we need to reach forward into a
new imaginary (or perhaps into an old imaginary?) of care.
This is the realm where the labour of care is conceptualised
as a commons, a shared endeavour for all people. In the
next two chapters, I take up the direct challenge of how to
bring that imaginary to life in practical, workable care initiatives that can also re-animate our caring commons.

Towards a Reformed
Care System

The focus of this chapter is on the professional social care system. In it, I will present a reformed yet fundamentally new model for how formal care may be delivered. While the proposals presented utilise the logic of the current system, this is done so that these suggestions are achievable and attainable. A more radical alteration would require a far more significant change in our underlying social model and theoretical framework. Given the urgency of the issues confronting us, and the critical lack of capacity of the system, we do not have the luxury of waiting for such a degree of change. I am proceeding based on the argument as set out above: our current care system is unable to adequately respond to our care needs, our care needs are growing and likely to greatly increase in the coming decades, and our wider social system is giving rise to a human subjectivity that is more vulnerable to factors which increase the need for care and yet, at the same time, is less likely to seek care. What will guide me is the methodological value offered by dialogue. In short, whatever system we wish to create, it must, to achieve both effectiveness and true liberation for those receiving care, be characterised by a genuine dialogic practice so that the metrics determining success or otherwise are co-produced by receivers of care.

One possible model is that offered by the feminist artist Cassie Thornton, which she has styled as *The Hologram*. While this approach has some limitations and itself is symptomatic of our deeper problems of disconnection, it nonetheless carries with it an operational viability and, at the same time, a utopian transcending of capitalism that I regard as apt for my purposes. My interest in *The Hologram* is that it is a practical instantiation of a dialogic model at work. I am not specifically championing *The Hologram* in itself. Rather, my concern is to present a minimum viable system that can be presented as an achievable and pragmatic model.

As we have seen, our current system, despite claims and protestations, is run for, and managed by, professional staff. The consequence is that the standards configuring how that work is done, and what constitutes success, are determined by a cadre of managers and policy makers. In dialogical systems, care givers and care receivers ideally *determine together* those standards. In blunt terms, care receivers need to equally decide what care they need and determine what resources they require to achieve this.

To address the immediate objection that this is overly aspirational and not realistic, let me reference briefly some existing dialogically based systems of professional care.

I have already noted the Open Dialogue approach used in the mental health service in northern Finland. This method is based on activating an immediate response to people in emotional distress through convening an open dialogue group comprised of the individual, their family and supporters, and at least two health care professionals. The approach, as outlined by Seikkula, involves:

(1) an immediate response by having the first meeting within 24 hours after contact; (2) a social networks perspective that in all cases invites relevant members of the client's social network and all the professionals involved in the actual crisis; (3) flexibility and mobility by always adapting to the unique needs of every client and family; (4) guaranteeing responsibility, so that whoever is contacted in the professional system becomes responsible for organizing the first meeting before any decision is made concerning the treatment; (5) psychological continuity by integrating staff from different services, like child psychiatry, outpatient mental health and so on, if needed – to work as an integrated team for as long as required; (6) tolerating uncertainty and generating a process for the new conversational community to 'live' and talk together; and (7) dialogicity as the primary aim in the joint meetings, to increase understanding about the actual crises and the life of our customers. By 'dialogism' I mean both responsive understanding and taking family members into explorations they would not otherwise undertake.[61]

This model, based on the principles of flexibility, person-centredness, integration of response, tolerance of uncertainty, working 'for as long as required' and dialogue, offers potential far beyond the confines of mental health issues. It also empirically demonstrates the operationality and functionality of a dialogue-based approach, given that the 'results' of this approach are demonstrably positive.[62] Critical though to the success of the Open Dialogue model in northern Finland has been the popular acceptance within the region of so radical a change, from a professional-led delivery to a dialogical determination of treatment responses. Drawing from these lessons we can conclude that the challenge in configuring our system of care is not so much architecture and design – it is as much a question of ethos and culture.

Another effort to introduce a more participative care model is that of Buurtzorg, which originated in the Netherlands.[63] This employs what is described as an 'onion' model, involving four layers: the self-managing client, informal support networks, the Buurtzorg team, and a formal support network. The core Buurtzorg team is made up of twelve care professionals who work in a community and get to know not only the individual receiving care but also their family, friends and supporters, as well as the care and medical professionals such as doctors, pharmacists, clinics, and so on. The team then offers a very person-centred relational model of care designed to fully mobilise these support resources. Here one can see the activation of both professional care and commons to provide a more holistic, situational care response for the individual.

In a manner similar to the Freirean pedagogue, the team first enculturate themselves locally, getting to understand the local community and its care resources, both formal and informal. The health care workers try not to be bound by care plans or targets but to be highly adaptive and responsive to the care needs of the individual as they emerge and change.

In citing these two initiatives I am not attempting any form of survey of possible care models. My concern is merely to show what is possible with dialogue as an orientation point. Before I outline *The Hologram* model, I wish to make two general qualifications. First, it must be acknowledged that care labour goes on all the time among 'actually existing' human beings. Indeed, the 'volume' of informal care greatly exceeds that of professional care by many factors. The model of formal care I am proposing does not in any sense seek to replace this. *The Hologram* is a model that can be implemented without any resources and therefore can act as a manifestation of the commons. However, it can also serve as a mode of operation for the care system. In short, it potentially can have one foot in the commons and one in a reformed, dialogic system. My focus for now is the system.

Secondly, the philosophy and practice of peer-to-peer care work is becoming more acknowledged. Specifically in the area of mental illness, much theoretical work has been done by scholars such as Mike Slade, Julie Repper and John Read.[64] A key assumption of the emerging recovery-based models of mental health care is the value of utilising lived experience as a support in working with people. The category of the peer support worker has emerged in recent years to designate somebody who can offer a peer relationship to a person experiencing health and care challenges. Currently in Ireland, there are two education programmes offering peer support qualifications.[65] Recovery colleges are another manifestation of this emerging paradigm. I have had close involvement with the first such college in the Republic of Ireland which began in 2014.[66] These colleges offer co-produced and co-delivered informal courses in health care and related issues where people's lived experience of these issues is accorded equal value to professional expertise.

In assessing the utility of *The Hologram* model I would like to keep these two points in focus, as they will remind us to observe an appropriate modesty that should frame our investigation (no model ever either creates care *de novo* or replaces actually occurring care) while also hinting at possibilities that may allow us to scale *The Hologram* beyond its current nascent application.

The Hologram

What then is *The Hologram*? Why am I selecting it for particular attention and why do I think the approach it offers might hold such transformative capacity and promise for care provision in twenty-first-century Ireland? For me, the potency of *The Hologram* is that it combines a highly practical, achievable and democratic model for immediate application with a rich conceptual underpinning that is a significant break from the logic and practice of commodified neoliberal social care. In elaborating this I will rely on Cassie Thornton's book *The Hologram: Feminist, peer-to-peer health for a post-pandemic future*, published in 2020. I also have had the benefit of completing a training programme on *The Hologram* facilitated by Cassie Thornton and others entitled *Building a New World from the Inside Out*. This title itself hints quite explicitly at the wider application intended by proponents of *The Hologram*.[67] It is not just a method for peer-empowered and -led care but also a mechanism for changing dominant socio-economic structures and relations.

Let us begin with a quick word on nomenclature.

> *The Hologram* refers to the project as a whole, whereas 'a Hologram' (capitalized but not italicized) names a group of four people, made up of a person, 'the hologram' (not capitalized) who receives the care of a 'triangle' of three people. This wording is intentionally ambiguous as it aims to sensitize us to the fluid boundaries between us.[68]

The core design is that one person receives the intentional care of three other people, chosen by the person, each of whom focuses on a specific dimension of the hologram's life: emotional, social and physical. The care takes the form of an attentive, dialogical engagement. There are two origin points in the development of the design. The first was Thornton's engagement as an artist (alone and sometimes in a collective called The Feminist Economics Department) on the theme of debt and how to make 'art about and against what capitalism does to our imagination'.[69] Her search was on how to address the negative and inhibiting effect of collective debt on the physical, mental and social health of individuals and collectives. The second was her encounter in 2017 with the solidarity clinics which had sprung up in Greece in response to the economic turmoil which had engulfed the country. Specifically, her interest was drawn to the Solidarity Health Clinic in Thessaloniki within which a collective called a Group for a Different Medicine had formed to organise aspects of the Workers' Health Centre. The centre categorised each person seeking care as an 'incomer' and encouraged them to become a member of the clinic's governing assembly. This participation was itself 'a central form of their health treatment'.[70] To further operationalise this, the centre put into practice four 'endeavours', one of which is called an 'integrative model':

> In this model, the incomer meets with three health practitioners at the same time on their first 90-minute visit: a general physician, a psychotherapist and a social worker or (if no social worker is available) a non-practitioner volunteer. The social worker (or volunteer) leads the incomer through a survey, called a health card, of optional questions covering their mental, emotional and physical health, but also

their broader situation, including their family life, living conditions, work, nutrition and sleep patterns; all are considered important aspects of health in a broad, holistic sense ... [T]hey are trying to make a hologram of every person: a clear three-dimensional image of health. This image not only benefits the care-givers, who now know the whole person, but also the incomer who can see themselves and their challenges more interdimensionally.[71]

As Thornton records:

As I sat in the Solidarity Clinic waiting rooms, talked with doctors, observed assemblies and accompanied incomers as they met with practitioners, I learned that most of the care given didn't need professional expertise – it was human connection, the provision of empathy and attention within what otherwise feels like an uncaring and alienating world where 'the crisis' becomes lodged in the body.[72]

What is striking in these observations is the discovery that when health care is not categorised as the preserve of a professional 'expert', 'medicine can become cooperatively creative and can actually produce multiple forms of mutually reinforcing "health": physical, emotional, social, communal and relational'.[73]

The Hologram proposal is intended as an explicit departure from the logic of neoliberalism. As well as a practical model which can be applied, it is also an exercise in breaking free from the constraints of capitalist subjectivity into the realm of a post-capitalist imaginary. Involved is a summoning up of an imagined future, an exercise in bringing a future possibility into the present, a time beyond capitalism. The intention is to create patterns for a post-capitalist now.

> At its broadest and most ambitious scale *The Hologram* is intended as an open-source, peer-to-peer, viral social technology for dehabituating humans from capitalism. Capitalism is not only an economic system, it's a cultural and social system as well, which deeply influences how we relate to one another, how we interact, how we imagine ourselves and one another, even how we talk and feel ... For this reason, in addition to the social practices involved in forming groups of four and doing the work of 'social holography', *The Hologram* is also a delivery mechanism for ideas about how we can reinvent our world by developing new daily habits that incorporate radical re-interpretations of these four themes: Trust, wishes, time, and patterns.[74]

These four themes address issues that expose how capitalism is internalised by the modern western subject and on how *The Hologram* marks a distinct break. I think it is worth examining each in turn before describing the actual working of *The Hologram*. Each not only describes cognitive-emotional features of our current system but, more specifically for my purposes in this book, points to quite distinct barriers to care giving and receiving.

As Wilkinson and Pickett and others have shown, levels of social trust are in serious decline in western societies generally.[75] Social capital theorists, following on from Putnam, have demonstrated how devastating to our health and well-being is the resultant loss of connection between people. If I can only trust myself and no-one else, then asking for trust or asking another to trust me is deeply uncomfortable. Simply asking someone to care for me outside of a transactional exchange is not only unorthodox but positively disturbing. Thornton addresses three toxic lessons about trust that need to be unlearned if a post-capitalist future is to be built.

The first is that our experience of institutional support is frequently bad. The formal care help we are offered is rarely unconditional or rarely without negative aspects. It can take more than it gives. Think of the onerous qualifying criteria to receive welfare or housing support, or the unsettling concept of being 'employable'. Not only must you be seeking a job, you must be 'passionate' even about the low-paid job you are seeking. The second lesson is that our dependence on systems, corporations or institutions causes us to

lose the skills and practices involved in asking for and offering help from people in our community. Having relationships where our central resources are carefully shared is fundamentally intuitive to humans, a cooperative species ... But when we do not actively practise sharing our resources we lose the muscles needed to do so, and we may even forget that this kind of hardcore interdependence is possible or desirable. Indeed, it can seem like a threat. Attention and care are also central resources and, while we all have the capacity to produce and receive them, it's not automatic and requires practice and structure.[76]

Finally, the third toxic learning is what she describes as 'failienation'.

If we feel that our inability to thrive is our personal responsibility and that we alone have failed (instead of realizing that the systems of support have failed all of us), we may not want to share our story or ask for help because we assume that we would be a burden on other people (if we assume they are not feeling like failures themselves). This is a self-defeating defense mechanism and often manifests in everyday life as being anti-social or even incurious toward others.[77]

The second 'de-programming' theme is that of wishes. One of the consequences of having unmet care needs in our conventional system is that one's personal wishes become either reduced or effectively eliminated. People can be so caught up in survival or endurance that they feel they do not deserve to have wishes, that wishes are not appropriate, that wishes are not possible, that they are not attainable anyway so why bother. They may seem like an indulgence, perhaps even dangerous because they may lead to inevitable disappointment. Even more alarmingly, are our wishes even ours or have we been somehow conditioned into certain wishes?[78] How can we find wishes for what we have not yet seen or can barely imagine?

The Hologram model seeks to reclaim genuine, human wishes.

> This project asks all participants to uphold a forceful optimism: we will survive better together. We can create a world where our wishes are contingent on each other's fulfillment, not on endless competition. And we suspect that the wishes we each have, when put together, can give us the energy and sustenance we need to engage in the ongoing crisis. We can solve each other's problems as we go toward our dreams, and getting closer to what we want will give us the energy to continue to deal with the never-ending list of emergencies. *The Hologram* is one methodology for unpacking our wishes; because I suspect that there is always a wish hiding below our wishes.[79]

The third issue needing de-toxification is time. We have already noted this feature as a critical resource rationed and controlled in a neoliberal care system. Freeing up time is a necessity for meaningful relationships. In care systems time is strictly managed and made subject to various performance metrics. Indeed, as I suggested above, wasting time is one of the greatest possible failures that can be attributed to a professional. As Thornton remarks: 'Under capitalism, time has become the most valuable commodity we have, outside of our body. As capitalism becomes more and more punishing and demanding, we have less and less time to imagine a different future. We've even heard people say that the ability to "imagine" something outside of work and survival is a "privilege".'[80]

To escape the regimented and colonised nature of capitalist time regimes, we need to be reminded of some fundamental truths. Thornton identifies what she designates as 'basic truths' which help break the entrancement of capitalist time.

1. Humans are fundamentally cooperative and interdependent.
2. We live on land and are part of that land.
3. We will die.

What would it mean to live without forgetting these truths? Our time would be very different. If we focused on learning how to cooperate without coercion we would have to reorganize what we produce, how we produce it, and why. If we acknowledged that we lived on land, and that land was alive, and that we are a part of it, we would laugh at the absurdity of the concept of private property. If we lived our whole lives embracing the knowledge that we will die we would better consider future generations as we made decisions. We might spend our whole lives carefully considering our uses of materials and time, knowing that our collective material and social traces produce the next generations' world. We would recognize that the now-dead once did so for our benefit. We would know that, when we die, we become each other's soil. If we remembered and believed these three truths how would we spend our time? What would our relationships look like? Where would we live and how? What would be our 'work' and how would we be valued?[81]

Based then on acknowledging these 'truths', *The Hologram* is a practice for liberating time. Inside *The Hologram* no-one is 'working', no-one is being measured or evaluated, no-one is engaged in a transactional exchange of value. Instead, what is occurring is simply the practice of care, freely given and freely accepted. Nothing must be done in return by the hologram receiving the care. There is no 'metric' determining the purpose or output of the task. *The Hologram* is not practical in the conventional sense. Instead, it requires that the participants are content to give time, or gift time to each other. The hologram chooses three people who would be prepared to meet as often as they agree to offer their time to them. The Hologram may last for years – indeed it is better if this is possible to allow the slow, deep engagement of a genuine human relationship of care. The arrangement is not transactional. The hologram receives care from the triangle but does not return it. However, they are responsible for encouraging and assisting each member of the triangle to select their own triangle of carers so they become care receivers also. Each person in the triangle should create their own Hologram. In this way, *The Hologram* organically grows throughout the society and develops as a counterweight to the system of care and even to capitalist reproduction.

The offering of time involved in *The Hologram* 'reveals your divestment from the accelerationist value system'.[82] As each member of the triangle forms their own Hologram, the individual hologram should in turn become a triangle member for someone else. Thus, the demarcation between care giver and care receiver breaks down. Everyone needs care. Everyone can give care. In this radicalised rupture from work and pay, a culture of care is revitalised and born deep within the liberated spaces of capitalism.[83] In the lexicon, you are both a hologram and you are triangular.

Finally, the fourth feature being disrupted here is what is designated as 'patterns'. The starting point is to recognise that our system generally, and systems of care more specifically, are breaking down. They are no longer serving. In this context there are many options. One is to keep patching up the system, but another is to support the destruction of what does not work. We have the choice also to create new, more dialogical and co-operative systems that will work in the unstable future that will soon be upon us. 'We can demolish in the night and rebuild in the morning.'[84]

The patterns of thought, hope, fear, relationships that we are habituated into reproduce the current system. Thus, to stop this occurring and produce a new system requires us to change these patterns of everyday socialisation.

> Of course, contrary to the new age, self-help industry's suggestion, simply believing something doesn't change reality, and that kind of individualism will only reproduce capitalism. Organizing and organization will be required, and we have the fight of our lives ahead of us. But a revolution like the one we need will not come about or stick unless we, as its participants, transform ourselves together. Changing our patterns and habits alone won't liberate us, but it will help us prepare for liberation, and for the world we will have to build.[85]

Let me now briefly describe the workings of the Hologram. While there is a protocol for how this is done, with very clear roles and structure, it should be noted that 'The Hologram remains a work in progress and is designed to be highly adaptable, so you are encouraged to change it and make it your own'.[86]

The hologram is the person seeking care. They invite three people of their choosing to make a formal commitment to supporting their health and care by agreeing to participate in regular meetings. Each one of the three invitees (the triangle) focuses on one dimension of the hologram's health – physical, emotional/mental and social. Each of these dimensions can be very broadly articulated so that, for example, physical may extend from the body of the hologram right up to the planetary environment as it impacts on them physically. Emotional and mental health can extend into frameworks of meaning and spirituality if that is of relevance to the hologram.

The core activity of the triangle is to ask questions. Therefore, their applied skill is simply curiosity. Curiosity is their expression of care. The purpose is not to offer answers or even to find answers in the questioning. It is simply to pose the questions. The answers and relevant expertise lie with the hologram. It can be seen how this system closely conforms to the dialogical model I outlined in The Dialogic Solution. The benefit for the hologram in this process is that they receive the questions as a gift which helps them discern and understand their own patterns and oppressions. Questions here become the beginning point of knowledge. A good, insightful question is the greatest gift of the triangle.

The meeting can last as long as the participants decide and can occur as often as they decide. The purpose is not to come to an answer or conclusion but perhaps to gain awareness of patterns. At a completely practical level, the triangle is simply a support. Maybe they may help the hologram prepare for a medical appointment or help them address a specific challenge occurring for them. They may help in teasing out information or allow them to clarify their own wishes and fears. In time, with repeated meetings, the triangle becomes a human record for the hologram. They come to know the hologram well and can help the hologram achieve perspective or personal agency.

> Unlike a patient being treated by a doctor, a hologram's role is like that of a teacher, helping the triangle to understand how she achieves her healthiest possible state and also recognize their own patterns, needs and wishes in contrast and conversation. The hologram shares her personal stories, her powers of communication and her well-articulated vulnerability to teach the triangle how to care for and with her.[87]

The protocol designed by Thornton and others sets out specific steps to guide the meeting. When the hologram and triangle are gathered, the first action is what is called 'the stuck dance'. Each member physically expresses in their body their experience of being 'stuck'. The hologram then sets the intention of the meeting, that is, she 'marks' the task, theme or topic for the discussion. This might include what is of concern to her at the moment, what she might wish to focus on in the meeting, and/or how she would like to be or to feel by the end. This serves as a type of guide for the triangle. The triangle then responds by posing open questions to the hologram, according to the particular dimension they have chosen. In this practice, questioning is the care practice. To pose questions to someone with compassion and attention and loving curiosity is a primordial act of care and a profound luxury in the time-poor and relationship-constrained world we daily experience. At the end of this there is time set aside for reflection or feedback. The hologram may speak about whether their intention or task has been met. Each triangle member may then record how they feel now that the dialogue is concluding. In addition, each of the triangle may respond to what they have heard in one of three ways. They may express a wish for the hologram, they may suggest a pattern in the hologram's thinking or behaviour which they have seen, or they may make a provocation by suggesting to the hologram, 'What if you did X or said Y, what would happen, or what would that feel like?' However, it is important to recognise that the triangle's role is not to suggest solutions or fix issues. It is quite straightforwardly to pose questions. It is a very pure dialogic practice. The ultimate purpose of the Hologram is to help the hologram make good decisions. It is not a therapy and not a mobilisation of 'expertise'.

The proposed conduct of *The Hologram* meeting is relatively straightforward.[88] Its potency however lies in how it breaks from the model of professionalised care, creates a true peer-to-peer engagement, restores social connection between otherwise atomised individuals, and offers the possibility for rapid expansion within the neoliberal social world. It is an evocation and manifestation of the caring commons and acts as an integral care labour in the sense in which I defined care in The Problem with Care as a liberation from what oppresses. In an essay in Thornton's book, Magdalena Jadwiga Härtelova situates *The Hologram* in participatory art, grassroots activism and radical thought. It is, she argues, an example of a 'post-work commons' and of a 'commons in exile'. As a post-work project, '*The Hologram* is a kind of revenge on capitalist time, its false scarcity and its perversions of value'.[89]

> In contrast to recent liberal and consumerist appro-priations of Audre Lorde's insistence on self-care as an act of political warfare, in *The Hologram* care is under-stood without any romantic or self-congratulatory flair. Rather, the project frames care as a dogged com-mon revolutionary practice, in the spirit of emancipa-tory, decolonial movements. *The Hologram*'s attention to the interdimensional material and psychological nature of oppression resonates with Frantz Fanon's analysis of colonialism as not only the physical but also the mental and social annihilation of oppressed people.[90]

The revolution imagined here is 'a revolution built on transformed relationships and the activity of committing time to building "worlds underneath this one"'.[91] This is both a recovery and creation of the commons, especially of the commons of care, which often lies hidden and dormant underneath the capitalist structure. Härtelova concludes:

Utopia marks a travel to a destination for the liberated imagination, an invitation to transformation, a portal. *The Hologram*, alongside many examples of anti-capitalist socially engaged art projects, is a collective exercise in radical re-imagination.[92]

Yet for all this *The Hologram* is not without limitation. No one model or method can of course be perfect. As I have remarked above, *The Hologram* is a symptom of the crisis we are in. It is an emergency response to a deficit of professional care resources. Its historical origin point after all is the Greek economic collapse. *The Hologram* comes into play precisely in a situation of a failure of the care system to meet the care needs of people. Its attraction lies in offering connection and response to individuals who have no material or financial resources to otherwise mobilise formal care. For many, it is a stopgap in a situation of disintegration.

The constraints however are not so much with the design of *The Hologram*. After all, it is simply what it is. The challenge is rather whether *The Hologram* can bear the weight that may be imposed upon it or whether it could achieve even more with redesign. Could we imagine escalating versions of *The Hologram*? Before engaging in Holograms 2.0 or 3.0 we do need to ask whether it is really possible to create a genuinely egalitarian dialogue community of four people. Can the hierarchies and cleavages of the social world be set aside within the dialogical space that it opens up? Can there genuinely be such 'liberated zones'? In the face of often compelling need, and real human suffering, can the triangle participants always voluntarily confine their role to that of compassionate curiosity? Might the temptation, even the appropriate response, be to intervene, to act, to change material circumstances on behalf of the hologram? Perhaps this too is possible within the evolving model. *The Hologram* values connection and meeting, but might sometimes action and doing be the appropriate mode of care response? Can *The Hologram* encompass cultural diversity and gender demarcations in diverse cultures where women talk better to women rather than to men, where older people may balk at seeking advice from the young? How would a hologram with intellectual disabilities or who is neurodivergent proceed, particularly if they did not communicate using words? These are perhaps just quibbles, as the flexibility of the model gives agency to the hologram to determine their triangle and proceed from there in terms of expectations.

What I now propose to do is to gather together what I have set out thus far and explore how we might construct a new, reformed care system in Ireland from these elements. I will be guided by the concern that we have a system that is truly dialogical, in particular one that permits care receivers to co-determine the intended outcome of care. The metrics of success must be co-produced between professional care givers and receivers. Might *The Hologram* model, if scaled up and revised, offer us a very practical template for how all of this may be done?

Care system

In the spirit of *The Hologram* we need at the outset to address two key questions: what needs to be destroyed and what needs to be created so that we can receive appropriate care? Currently, despite the personal motivations and ethics of the individuals working within the care system, our care model acts largely as a short-term emergency response to the multiple victims of our social world. As we have seen, not only is the current system a limited balm attempting to bind up the consequences of a careless reality, it is increasingly misshapen by neo-liberal values, manifesting themselves in marketisation, consumerisation and managerialisation. What we need is a model that is a distinct and real departure from this system and one that constitutes a tangible movement towards a more caring world.

In The Dialogic Solution, I identified three fundamental problems with our contemporary care system. These were that a vast number of new care demands or needs being produced by our disintegrating social world are not being addressed by the care system because it does not recognise them in the first place (issues such as loneliness, meaninglessness, alienation, eco-despair) or is simply being overwhelmed by the sheer scale of presentations.

Our market-based system cannot deal with them – indeed it largely creates them. Inequality, exclusion, homelessness, addiction, and so on give rise to a veritable overwhelming tide of care need. The second problem therefore is that the commodified care system produced by neoliberalism cannot offer an adequate response to these care and health issues. There simply are not enough resources to respond adequately to every care need. Hence, we either have no service available at all or else long waiting periods for services. In either case, this is an inimical situation for care. The level of human suffering increases and finds little relief. Finally, our wider social world posits a subjectivity that makes looking for care, and being dependent on care, a negative signifier of one's utility and value. In a world centred on individual success, where there are no social problems only bad personal choices, the care-seeking individual feels like a 'loser' who is a drain on hard-earned taxpayers' money. The very inadequacy of the system becomes re-fashioned as a useful negative incentive discouraging individuals from 'dependency' and orienting them back towards responsibilisation. Of course, no-one would dare put it in such explicit terms but this is what is experienced by so many people. 'Really existing' human beings know that the constructed subjectivity of the self-interested, rational, utility-maximising actor is an ideological creation that hits its limit conditions as soon as care needs emerge.

Care then becomes a fissure in the façade of neoliberal artifice. I suspect this very fissure is at the root of much additional distress when people become ill or need care as adults. If I am not working, not earning, then who am I? The image of myself as one dependent on others is highly disconcerting. Hence, people may *de facto* collude with professionals to be returned to social functionality as rapidly as possible by quick pharmaceutical or surgical interventions rather than take the time for full recovery or to explore the deep reasons for illness or distress. We have entire industries of self-help and self-care designed to keep us 'balanced' in our work or to get us back to productive endeavour as soon as possible.

To design a new care system we need therefore to address each of these problems. In short, the three issues we need any care system to tackle are those of demand (care needs), supply (care response), and the subjectivities either degrading or accentuating care. For a reformed system to be viable it must better resolve these than the current model.

In summary, the proposal I wish to outline is to make dialogue the meta-metric guiding all care provision. Every care service must acknowledge dialogue as its operational methodology. Critically, this means that care receivers are included dialogically in determining how the outcome of the care service is to be measured. What would constitute success? This key mode of neoliberal management must be inflected progressively through care receivers co-producing the metrics determining completion and outcome. Outcome becomes a democratically agreed product between deliverer and receiver.

In this way, the very logic of the market (where, after all, the consumer is meant to be sovereign) is followed to its syllogistic conclusion – the care receiver decides.

The second step is to take *The Hologram* as a skeleton model for actualising a dialogical and holistic care service. *The Hologram* is designed within a zero-resource setting but what if it was resourced? Could the radical model offered of a three-dimensional, holographic perspective on the person, within a dialogical process, be extended to encompass how the care system might in fact be structured? Would we not have a radical and progressive transformation if access to a scaled-up Hologram model was made a legal right? This change, combined with the mandatory metric of dialogue, would profoundly change our care system.

Finally, we need deep social healing and cultural recovery from the ravages wrought on us by growth-centred capitalism. This system has reached its endpoint. It cannot continue in its present form without complet-ing a vast destruction of life on Earth. In the context of care, the recovery process requires a re-mobilisation and re-accessing of the social and ecological commons. This is clearly a large question. I will address this briefly in the final chapter by examining the creative potential offered by a universal basic income.

To bring all this together in one sentence, my proposal then is to have an Irish care system characterised by dialogue as a mandatory meta-metric, delivered through a legally enforced Hologram-styled model, and grounded in a commons of care better resourced through a basic income available to all.

Dialogue

The value and model of dialogue has been described in The Dialogic Solution above. I do not wish to dwell too much further on it. However, dialogue is more than merely a pragmatic mode of communication. The act of truly listening and empathically responding to the word of another (whether that is through language, gesture or behaviour) activates deep capacities in the human person. More to the point, the experience of being heard and responded to is a profoundly humanising one. It is a recognition of each person's subjectivity, that I have something of value to contribute, that I matter, that I too have a point of view requiring respect. So much of today's poor care experiences are the result not only of inadequate *resources* but of inadequate *response*, the sense of not being heard. As we all know, our greatest frustration arises from not being listened to. This is what relegates us to the position of the object, the one who is acted upon by the subject-who-knows. In dialogue, two or more subjects meet and together agree on what the issue to be addressed is and how it will be done. There is a central role here of course for the professional but the professional is required to be a participant in a collective act of care situated with others.

The only way to move this beyond piety and aspiration is to programme dialogue into the very metrics by which contemporary care is measured. If we must have evaluation and performance indicators, then let mandatory dialogue as judged by the care receiver be central. There are many models for doing this – pre-interview cards, compulsory checklist of topics beyond the presenting issue, co-produced care and treatment plans. The requirement for dialogic practice can be built into the service level agreements by which many care providers are funded by the state and the HSE. Equally, HIQA's and the Mental Health Commission's evaluations of residential centres and other services could prioritise the centrality of dialogic practice by seeking evidence of residents' committees, co-evaluation procedures and dialogic culture at all levels of care provision. Dialogue, genuinely manifested, is profoundly democratic.

The point here is that dialogue is more than an instrument of care. The very process of dialogue is itself therapeutic.[93] So, not only is dialogue a way to respond to care needs (supply), it reduces those needs in the long-term (demand) by restoring social connection, mutuality and subject-recognition to people.

Finally, the subversive nature of such an approach should not be underestimated. As I noted above in The Dialogic Solution, giving people the ability to co-produce the care outcomes they need is quite likely to open up outcomes such as housing, income and other welfare and support requirements. Often people do not need medication, they need a home, or a basic income. Often, too, they do not need to manage stress and anxiety through exercise or mindfulness, they just need secure material living circumstances. Care then may be forced out of its current comfortable service provision enclave and into the contesting realm of politics and social activism. Irish care in this way may become less about containing human suffering within a limited social system and more about changing that system in the first place. Care work thus may transition from being largely confined to the inter-personal realm and into the socio-political arena. Would we be able to recognise such activism as in fact care work? This would raise challenges for the professional cadre as well as for educational institutions and regulatory bodies such as CORU. What would the core skills of the social care worker be in a dialogically informed, politically active profession?

Scaled-up *Hologram*

Could *The Hologram*, or a version of it, serve as a model for the delivery of professional care services? In other words, could it allow us to operationalise the requirement for dialogue and provide a viable vehicle for directing the care service towards democratic inclusion? What would it look like if it were resourced? The table below illustrates the possible applications of such a flexibly scaled structure of care.

LEVEL	MODE	COMPOSITION
Pre-Level	Emergency	Peer Support / Professional
Level 1	Informal	Peer-to-peer
Level 2	Semi-formal	Peer Support Workers
Level 3	Formal	Professionals

Table 1: Schema of integral dialogic care using a *Hologram* model

In its current design *The Hologram* is an entirely peer-to-peer system. The hologram calls forth three people to act as their triangle. If we were to add resources, could we imagine an escalating tiered Hologram model that inserted itself into the very care system itself? A Level 1 Hologram might therefore be its current iteration – an entirely peer-to-peer informal network used as required by the individual hologram, set up by that person and needing no permission or resources to do so. A Level 2 Hologram might be one where the peers utilised by the individual hologram are trained or certified peer support workers, available as part of the system's service provision. This does not mean they are better than 'pure peers'. It just means that they have completed some training or education in peer support practice to better equip themselves to be of benefit to a hologram peer. They are still not claiming expertise and not setting out to resolve or 'fix' issues. Their value is as a standing and available resource for those potential holograms who cannot easily access three peers from their own networks who would have the time or other capacity to be available as required. In other words, these peer support workers form an available cohort of human care resources which can be mobilised by putative holograms. We can think of great numbers of people in Ireland currently who do voluntary work to provide peer help to others. Consider the numbers involved in suicide prevention on bridges, those who fundraise for mental health and physical health supports, and so on. There is a potentially large number of people who, given an available and flexible model, might be prepared to serve as peer hologram supports.

Finally, at a possible Level 3, the care and medical system could itself be structured as a Hologram. What if an individual had a legal right to have a three-person care team (or more) made up of diverse and relevant professionals who were involved in their care? What if they had a right to meet with the professional trio to review dialogically their care situation, their care plan, and to co-produce the metrics that would determine outcome and success? At a minimum, this tripartite engagement would remove the infamous 'dual diagnosis' problem where someone who has two distinct medical diagnoses is placed on parallel tracks of care without these being integrated, even though for the individual concerned it may all be the one connected issue. The classic example is someone with an addiction issue and a mental health diagnosis. Or what about a cancer patient who needs bio-medical treatment but also counselling and well-being support, as well as nutritional and exercise advice? At this imagined Level 3 the care receiver could seek an integration of care among the relevant professionals. In turn, the professionals must learn to coordinate and combine and perhaps recognise how their preferred care strategy might conflict with the other professional approaches. All other things being equal, this should result in a far better care experience for the receiver and a far better care service even from the professionals' perspective. The chances are that better co-ordination would lead to better use of resources. Listening to colleagues' different perspectives would likely enhance the care response. The therapeutic benefits of the care receiver being included in the care planning and assessment are considerable. The principle remains that once you are addressed as a subject and not an object, your well-being is greatly enhanced. In consequence, your immune system will function better and your chances of recovery or wellness are significantly improved.

In addition, there may be an argument for a further level of *The Hologram* application. There are of course cases where people have emergency needs or go into periodic crisis. Rather than having to wait for the meeting of one's informal, semi-formal or professional Hologram, there may be a need for a type of emergency response Hologram made up of peer support workers or professional social or health care workers who can quickly mobilise to provide an immediate tripartite dialogic response. I am not speaking here of course of someone in a medical emergency but rather of those who need an immediate activation of support before an issue escalates. This may arise for someone experiencing a significant stress event or emotional distress, or someone who may need immediate advice or support on some specific emerging issue. The value being applied here is that early intervention offers the best mode of response rather than allowing an escalation into a greater or more complex challenge. In all of these cases the opportunities now opened up by the internet for online meetings makes this architecture of immediate dialogic care far more possible.

Structuring the care system on a dialogic model such as that exemplified in *The Hologram* would be a significant break in the standard operation of the current neoliberal system. It would place the individual genuinely at the centre of care and would seek to mobilise care resources around that individual with an escalation to professional inputs only if required. Once again, the key assumption is that social connection is in itself therapeutic and, accordingly, being offered the space and time to talk through issues is inherently helpful. If this is done as soon as possible, as either an early or preventative intervention, then many issues need not develop into problems which would require far more detailed and expensive responses later. The generative ethic of dialogue within such a model, where outcomes of care are co-produced, would provide a powerful counterthrust to today's dominant and constrained system.

The Commons of Care

As indicated at the outset, my primary concern is to sketch a practical and achievable picture of a more caring Ireland, integrating both a reformed system of care and a renewed commons of care. While *The Hologram* model is offered as a potential instantiation of a better-functioning *care system* in the sense of one that produces more care, the broader goal is to transform both system and society towards better recognising the human being as a dialogical subject.

The connection between care system and care commons is complex and multi-faceted. In one sense, the system is dependent on the commons and serves only as an adjunct to the vast labour of care manifested in the commons. We turn to the system when commons' resources fail us or are inadequate to resolve the care and health needs that present. In another sense though, the system can act to displace the commons by seeking to transfer the practice of care as relationship between connected subjects into care as commodity performed by professional actors. In imagining a new caring Ireland, we need to achieve a far better balance in which system complements and supports commons. *The Hologram* is one interlinking possibility, in that it offers a reform of the system as well as an animation of the commons. In this final chapter, I want to suggest a further structural change which attempts an additional fusion between system – not just the care system but the social welfare system more generally – and the caring commons. The proposal for a universal basic income (UBI) seeks to respond directly to a number of the causes of care needs that this book has identified – material inequality, social disconnection, neoliberal subjectivity, maldistribution of care labour and the marginalisation of the caring commons. Were a UBI to be adopted, combined with the dialogical re-structuring of the care system, then I think we would have a solid foundation for a more caring Ireland, in which system and commons combine in a more symbiotic and reinforcing way. The objective ultimately is to affirm and develop the dialogical and relational human subject, by ensuring that we have a system in service to such a subject, and by encouraging the growth of a commons in which the subject may holistically prosper.

Before outlining this proposal, I want to once more briefly describe this subject so that our task is clear. The subject of care affirmed in this book is the one whose very embodiment requires the exchange of care, both giving and receiving, as an inherent aspect of their being. Care here is understood not to be reliant on an emotion nor even on a 'choice' exercised in the current mode of the authenticity-seeking self, but rather as a commitment to the needs of the other due to my relationship to them. Personal desire gives way to the far more profound human requirement to exercise responsibility and faithfulness to the other with whom I am in relationship. In this sense, the optimum way to unmask the illusory autonomous self of contemporary neoliberal ideology is in fact through the practice of care. Indeed, far more ambitiously, the solution to our current inability, or unwillingness, to respond to our multiple social and ecological crises, exemplified in the political challenge of how the neoliberal subject could possibly live within limits that are self-chosen, lies precisely in the practice of care. This wider question of care being a life lived within limits for the good of others must be addressed because we currently exist in the 'tragic space' between our failing dominant social system (which is no longer fit for use) and a new system yet unborn. Unbridled economic growth, based on desire-maximising consumption, is no longer a viable form of life. The journey from the sovereign self to the relational self must move through the recognition of limits as an act of care for others. This privileging of care as a route into voluntary limits is both empirical (observe the response to the illness or disability of a loved one or our collective response to communal tragedy) and normative (we know it is what we ought to do in the face of human fragility, dependency and materiality).

The commons of care

In exploring the challenge of limits, and thus voluntary sacrifice as an act of solidarity, there arises the operational and conceptual inspiration offered by a recovery of the commons. This is because the labour of human care, within what we might designate as the wider ecology of care, is fundamentally a work of commoning. Commons here is used not as a noun but a verb. The commons of care refers then to the vast work of care carried out by really existing human beings which gives rise to human sociality and relationality. If we are to set out a path for a renewed caring Ireland, then we must turn our attention to this task of commoning care so that we can not only recover our capacity to see it but, far more importantly, to value it and enhance it so that it can be the foundation of our shared social and ecological world. We have rendered largely invisible and of low value the vast work of care that characterises our caring commons. This has particularly marginalised women, especially poorer women.

The argument, I hope, is straightforward. What we ultimately need in order to ensure our humanity and our planet is a caring world. A caring world is a world of maximum relationality. Creating a relational care system and wider commons of care is simply an imperative for our time.

My proposal with the care system set out in Towards a Reformed Care System therefore was to try to shift it into a more relational mode, one that is more compatible with, and respectful of, human subjectivity. Our humanity needs re-asserting in this way because we in the modern West have been living within one of the narrowest conceptions of what it is to be human of any culture that we know of. The Cartesian subject believes that they end at their skin and beyond that point is 'the other' or 'the environment'. Hence, we become the 'anxious monad' referenced by Eilís Ward, looking out at a world of objects from within the limited horizon set by our isolated individuality.[94] If the individual is pronounced author of their own privatised world, then what becomes of primary value are my own thoughts, my own desires, my own self-identifications. Into this solipsistic void marches the Nietzschean proposal that in a world without external morality or objective truth there is only power, the sheer unencumbered will of the *overman* who has the strength to impose his own order. Sartrean existentialism elevates individual choice as the authentic means by which the individual can be who they really want to be. Self-realisation becomes a socially affirmed goal to be achieved by the exercise of personal freedom. The colonisation of this by capitalism directs freedom towards fulfilment of desire attained through consumption. The consequent elevation of private *eros* drives the individual into the relentless pursuit of personal satisfaction so that the ultimate goal of life – the new superego injunction to be happy – can be achieved.

As Barbara Ehrenreich bluntly put it – you must either smile or die. In this way we become intolerant of the unhappy, the needy, the 'losers', disturbed by their failure to correct themselves into the new order of being.[95]

This is the ideological context within which care labour in the commons is being ever more relegated and displaced by inadequately resourced care commodities. The careless world that has resulted is now coming to claim us. Environmental breakdown and all the resultant social and political upheavals are about to engulf us. The stark reality before us is that we will either care or die.

This narrowing of the human has become a form of enclosure, so that we can now speak of the neoliberal individual as an *enclosed self*. The enclosed self is bound and confined by the material and conceptual limits set by the capitalist order and imaginary. The way out is by the practice of commoning, within which the commoning of care is surely central.

The care commons refers to, first, the vast affective care domain of ordinary life which 'gives people direction and purpose in their daily lives and is central to how they define themselves'.[96] This includes the domains of family, friendship, inter-personal relationships, work, school, community, clubs, and so on where people interact caringly with each other. Secondly, it refers to all that conscious care practice or love labour that people perform for each other outside of any commodity exchange or payment or professional practice. Neither of these manifestations of the care commons is integrated directly into the enclosures of capitalism.

Though the notion of the commons is often associated with either the work of Elinor Ostrom or with various counter-currents to her institutional framing which emphasises the political and emancipatory potential of commons as an alternative to the state and private corporations, I wish to emphasise commons as a practice which constructs social reality. In his 2014 article 'Commoning in the New Society' in the *Community Development Journal*, Gustavo Esteva cites Peter Linebaugh's observation that:

> [t]o speak of the commons as if it were a natural resource is misleading at best and dangerous at worst, the commons is an activity and, if anything, it expresses relationships in society that are inseparable from relations to nature. It might be better to keep the word as a verb, rather than as a noun, a substantive.[97]

Esteva indicates four features of the 'social commons' that he sees emerging: their diversity, that they are social relationships, that they are not resources and not therefore defined by ownership, and that they are realistic.

> Both scholarly scrutiny and empirical experience are evidencing that the dominant system cannot deal with the current crises. It lacks realism to continue

expecting that conventional paths will deliver what we urgently need. As the Zapatistas say, to change the world is very difficult, perhaps impossible; what seems feasible is to create a whole new world. This is what the people are doing, all over the world, through commoning.

The time has come to enclose the enclosers. Commoning, commonism, reclaiming, and regenerating our commons and creating new commons, beyond the dominant economic and political system, define the limits of the current era.[98]

Reconnecting with our caring commons – by acknowledging its inherent value, by creating social networks, by acting dialogically (such as in *The Hologram* or other models) – restores communion between human subjects and offers us a path away from the enclosed self. As I have suggested throughout, in our neoliberal world the enclosed self longs for care but cannot access it sufficiently and is furthermore losing the ability to even ask for it. Commoning allows us to regain our agency in responding to the needs and vulnerabilities of each other. It is a form of radical activism by which the world can be shaped anew. The UBI proposal is intended to enhance that agency through economic resourcing.

I think it important to emphasise what exactly is at stake in this reclamation of our caring commons. The separation between people enforced by liberal humanism is an enclosure *sine qua non*. The divisions emergent within modernity sundered connection, escalated pre-modern social cleavages into new, more entrenched forms, and fractured solidarities and supports of care and bonds characteristic of the commons. The enclosure of physical space went side by side with the imposition of psychological and moral enclosures between human subjects. The enclosed self of modernity became the disconnected self, the divided self, with new fissures opened between human and other-than-human, between the secular and the sacred, male and female, modern and traditional, rational and affective, the sane and the mad, the self and the other, mind and body, subject and object. Instead of mutuality there was separation, instead of co-operation there was competition, instead of commoning relationship there were the binaries of enclosure.

Commoning then, especially the commoning work of care, becomes a project of re-integration, outside the logics of the market and utility maximisation. Care relocates the human subject into relationality and subverts the entire artifice of isolated self-interest. As I have repeated above, the very materiality of the human body breaks the illusion of autonomy. Not only does the care-needing body pronounce a claim, our response, indeed our compulsion to respond to the suffering of another person, draws us out of our enclosed self into encounter, into reconnection. In this precise way, the claim of the care demand requires for authentic response the subjectivity of the care giver acknowledging the subjectivity of the care receiver. In place of monologue, we see dialogue.

This then is the utopian objective in the revival of the caring commons. In the face of the social and ecological challenges before us, combined with the pressure exerted by our severely ill-equipped care system, we must place our feet once again on the firm ground of our shared commons. The care system then can act as an augmenter and supporter of the care capacities already in play.

Joan Tronto's book *Caring Democracy: Markets, equality, and justice* sets out to describe how a caring political state might look. She responds to the same challenge that I have set out here:

> Humans begin and end their lives depending upon others for care; in between those times we never cease being engaged in relationships of care with others, and we never cease needing and providing care for ourselves. As our interdependence in caring grows greater, we need to rethink how we parse out our time, energy, work, and resources to make certain that we, as well as those around us, are well cared for. We cannot rethink these questions in isolation, we can only do so collectively. And in so doing, we will change how we see ourselves in the world and what should guide our most fundamental political choices.[99]

Her book outlines a number of practical policy, political and social changes that, she argues, better support the labour of care and the capacity to receive care.

> The starting principle with which this renegotiation must take place is this: We have got things backwards now. The key to living well, for all people, is to live a care-filled life, a life in which one is well cared for by others when one needs it, cares well for oneself, and has room to provide for the caring – for other people, animals, institutions, and ideals – that gives one's life its particular meaning. A truly free society makes people free to care. A truly equal society gives people equal chances to be well cared for, and to engage in caring relationships. A truly just society does not use the market to hide current and past injustices. The purpose of economic life is to support care, not the other way around. Production is not an end in itself, it is a means to the end of living as well as we can. And in a democratic society, this means everyone can live well, not just the few.[100]

Primarily, her concern is to circumvent the various 'passes' by which certain people or classes of people evade their care responsibilities. She argues cogently that we need to move beyond the gendered, racialised and class-laden maldistribution of care responsibilities to ensure that the labour of care is properly supported and valued and is the proper responsibility of all. Thus, the work of protection (policing, prisons), of economic production, of direct care (not only for 'my own' but for all) and of economic life must be directed to producing care, not harm and oppression. To achieve all of this requires an activist, democratic, political project which re-centralises care. For Tronto, 'it is clear now that making caring a central value in democratic life will require a rethinking of many existing social institutions, political institutions, and practices'.[101]

The proposal for a UBI is one effort to respond to this challenge of the marginalisation and maldistribution of care work. As I noted in The Problem with Care, UBI pays carers for the work they do, frees them from economic dependency on others within the family network or from the need to engage in low-paid or precarious employment, and, by this financial resourcing, makes the performance of domestic care tasks more a matter of election than necessity. The objective is that this should permit a far greater equalisation of who undertakes care roles and of the social and economic status attached to those roles.[102] By this means, the care and welfare systems can become supporters of the commons-situated labour of care. Tronto's concern that the labour of care is supported and valued can thereby be better achieved.[103]

As our subjectivity has been crudely narrowed in neoliberalism, so too has our circle of care. Too often, we may limit our caring response to those immediately about us – our family rather than all families, our country rather than all countries, my species rather than all species. At one level this necessary boundary is explicable, as within the economy of care I cannot literally respond to all potential care claims on me. Yet, nonetheless, for the commoning of care to express its full potentiality to transform the relational subject, we need an assertion of a truly inclusive, universal care value. The philosopher Josef Pieper offers one possible articulation when he defines love as saying to the other: 'It is good that you exist; it is good that you are in the world.'[104] This formulation not only transcends the uncaring distinction between worthy and unworthy lives, the valuable and the discarded human, it asserts a positive standard affirming life itself. This principle of affirmation is critical in establishing value for the disabled, the otherwise unwanted, the oppressed and marginalised, the other-than-human.[105] Crucially, the recognition of intrinsic value imposes an obligation to defend and uphold that value. It is this that moves care away from the narrow realm of the emotive response into the realm of the disciplined responsibility, from empathic feeling into intentional sacrifice. We may be reminded of Buber's declaration that love is the *responsibility* of an I for a Thou.

The concern of this book has been to outline in achievable terms what a more caring Ireland might look like. How might we better facilitate the cultural transformation from the enclosed self to the commoning self? How might our social care and welfare systems be structured to build upon, and enhance, the caring commons?

One guiding principle to orient us in responding is that, all other things being equal, social connection leads to better health and social outcomes. The greater the disconnection, the greater the health and social challenges. Connection refers not just to the density of social relations but also to what extent our dominant social frameworks of meaning enhance our relationships. Authentic relationships require a caring orientation. For them to be real, I must be concerned with how the other is and invested in their well-being. Thus, it can be seen how inimical, indeed actively destructive, to care is a perspective of human engagement centred on utility, self-interest and commodity exchange.

We see evidence of this damage all around us. The *Planet Youth* surveys of transition-year students in the west of Ireland provide a rich insight into the experiences of our fifteen–sixteen-year-olds.[106] This cohort serves as a mirror of wider social processes but also as a predictor of issues to come. In Mayo, the 2022 survey reported that 41.4 per cent of girls and 22.4 per cent of boys have self-harmed once or more. A third have considered suicide, with 9.3 per cent having made an attempt to do so. Almost 30 per cent of boys and 60 per cent of girls said they would benefit from help with mental health issues. It seems clear that great numbers of our young people experience the world as difficult, indeed overwhelming. The competitive, autonomous, falsely positive project of personal happiness is simply not working for growing numbers. We appear to be inhabiting both a devastated inner and outer world.

Universal basic income

It seems reasonable to claim that our current system of care is oriented towards symptom response. As has been outlined above, this can never be adequate, as the resources available cannot meet the demand for care, and this approach ignores the causes producing care needs in the first place. A re-set is needed whereby the care system becomes a complement to a renewed commons of care. As I have suggested, *The Hologram* model points to one possible direction for the professional social and health care system. Care receivers become co-producers of their own care and professionals become facilitators of care rather than knowing subjects acting on receiving objects.

The proposal that there be a universal basic income would build on this systemic change by attempting to incorporate the social welfare system into this wider transformation of supporting and enhancing the caring commons. It does so by better addressing the sources of many care needs and by better resourcing individuals to respond to those needs. It also further activates the social and caring commons ('the commons in exile') by encouraging and facilitating new forms of creativity and connection. At the outset it should, however, be acknowledged that UBI on its own is not a silver bullet. For it to be truly transformative, it needs at a minimum to be combined with more accessible and affordable state services so that low income ceases to be a barrier to public resource provision. In short, a basic income must be a living wage, genuinely allowing for an adequate mobilisation of health and care resources.

Basic Income Ireland defines UBI as: 'the proposal that the state should make a regular payment to every individual resident regardless of circumstances, without any means test or work requirement. It would be enough to live a frugal but decent life without additional income'.[107] They cite three main reasons why this would be of benefit: it produces a more caring society, it improves quality of life, and it creates a more dynamic economy.[108]

Perhaps the most comprehensive treatment of this concept is in Philippe Van Parijs and Yannick Vanderborght's book *Basic Income: A radical proposal for a free society and a sane economy*.[109] They stress the universal or unconditional element of the proposal. By this they mean the payment is made to each individual resident in a particular, territorially defined community. It is not linked to household situation or to specific need or circumstance. This individual approach greatly affects the distribution of power within the household as it impacts directly on financial dependency and related issues. The payment is universal also in the sense that it is not tied to income or to any means test. Finally, it is obligation-free. No work or any other action is required in exchange for its receipt. Again, as we saw above with *The Hologram*, no transaction or reciprocation dynamic is in play to merit the payment.

The payment amount could vary with age (more could be given for the elderly, less for children), geography (some areas may have unique additional costs associated with living there) or time (it could be linked for example to inflation or changes in GDP). While the payment is basic, nonetheless it is 'a foundation on which one can stand because of its very unconditionality'.[110]

How much income are they suggesting? Their proposal is that a basic income should be set at 25 per cent of per capita GDP. Thus, for Ireland, a quick calculation indicates that, in 2022, using OECD per capita figures,[111] a basic income would be €29,308.86.[112] Their book goes into great detail on addressing objections, design issues and cost and funding issues. These proofs of viability or otherwise are not our immediate concern here.

What is of relevance to us is the transformative impact of a UBI on the caring commons. It helps by, in effect, paying caring commoners. It resources individuals, supports families in all of their multiple forms, facilitates caring networks and energises communities, all of which enhances the relational connection between people and releases caring resources outside the formal system of care. Noting again that the full effectiveness of UBI also requires state services and policies to support communities and commons, and of course a reformed care system operating dialogically and symbiotically with the commons, nonetheless we can identify at least four specific benefits to a UBI provision in Ireland which directly impact on the commons of care.

1. Alleviates material poverty

The most apparent benefit is the potential for a direct impact on reducing economic poverty. The UBI provides a secure floor of income. Individuals are free to then work in paid employment if they wish or not. Additional income is retained, subject to taxation, but the UBI is guaranteed irrespective of their employment status. This allows people to say no to bad and precarious jobs. It frees them from the unemployment and employment trap. 'The former facilitates saying yes to a job offer, while the latter facilitates saying no.'[113] Rather than the plethora of contingent and means-tested welfare payments, combined with the *de facto* penalising of people who enter low-paid employment, the UBI offers security and an economic dignity irrespective of market integration or functionality. In addition, it frees people from the economic and indeed social pressure to be involved in the precarious and 'bullshit' jobs[114] so endemic in our neoliberal economy. It allows for a reduction of the often pejorative distinction between work and wage-labour. Almost everybody 'works' but not everyone is always 'employed'.

As we know, the greatest single cause of social and health problems is inequality. UBI helps to better equalise social status and inclusion. This reduces the corrosive effect of material deprivation and consequent shame and stigma. The cruel dynamic of a society of winners and losers is at least alleviated. Crucial to its impact is that basic income significantly reduces the many economic pressures which act as disintegrators of social connection.

2. Acknowledges care labour

By de-coupling income from labour, the UBI in effect financially rewards the care work performed by so many in the commons of care. This payment would thereby free people to devote themselves to full-time care if they so choose, rather than being obliged by necessity to combine domestic care work with external employment. This would be of additional benefit to primary care givers who might wish to parent full-time or part-time but feel constrained in doing so due to financial pressures. Resourcing families in this way to support the young, the elderly and the ill would have an enormously positive effect on the caring commons.

Despite neoliberalism's implicit project of atomisation and breaking down of collective endeavours, the family in all of its forms remains as a core site of care labour. It is into a family after all that the utterly vulnerable human infant is born and can only survive if cared for. The dynamics of care between infant and its primary care givers – the quality of attachment, of emotional attunement, of relational response – in a literal sense configures the very structure of the developing brain.[115] The stressed care giver – whether due to economic, social or psychological factors – quite understandably struggles to meet the care needs of dependent children. The issue before us is not moral or personal failure, it is systemic. In particular, the gendered marginalisation of the care labour of women, drawn on the patriarchal assertion that care is primarily a woman's task and the domestic space a preferentially female habitat, is a structural feature that seeks to reduce both the status of women and the value of care labour. If we are to support a culture of care in twenty-first-century Ireland, we must pay close attention to supporting the family, including addressing these gendered and economic pressures, so that the work of care is open to all and not maldistributed to a vulnerable cohort of dependent and financially insecure people, whose work of care renders them even more marginal.

3. Rejuvenates community

As I have acknowledged above, *The Hologram* can itself be seen as a symptom of social disintegration. Its emergence signals the failure of more traditional networks of connection between people such as friendship bonds or familial, communal or work-based associations. *The Hologram* points to a situation where individuals must make a conscious effort to identify others who will listen to them. In this sense, care is called forth through an act of will. For many, the social world is not offering structures or settings within which relational interactions offer sufficient support or engaged dialogue. Recall here the man I referenced in *The Dialogic Solution* – 'Who do I speak to? And what do I say to them?' The Hologram's triangle is almost a substitute for lack of friendship.

It seems clear that we need to build a commons resource for denser social connections between people in order to enhance the quality of care between us. While Ireland may not yet be quite on a par with many of our European neighbours, loneliness and isolation are growing. Findings from the Irish Longitudinal Study on Ageing published in 2019[116] show that almost a third of adults over fifty years of age experience emotional loneliness. The consequent effect on mental health seems evident in studies such as TASC's 2023 report *Is an EU-Wide Approach to the Mental Health Crisis Necessary?* which indicates that up to 42 per cent of Irish people meet diagnostic requirements for at least one mental health challenge.[117]

What is puzzling here is that, as social primates, we are hard-wired for sociality. Once more, it seems that our unique social system is interfering with that fundamental need in us and forcing us apart. Access to a UBI would permit people to freely engage in community projects of all kinds, unencumbered by the need to derive an income from such activities. In this way, the pressure of capitalist social relations is reduced in favour of commoning relations. One can readily anticipate the proliferation of community enhancement projects and the creation of communal networks based on mutual interest, support and enjoyment. Rutger Bregman's popular book *Humankind: A hopeful history* reminds us: 'It wasn't the invisible hand of the market that gently shepherded peasants from their farms into factories, but the ruthless hand of the state, bayonet at the ready. Everywhere in the world, that "free market" was planned and imposed from the top down.'[118]

It seems clear that, if we are to activate our commons of care, we need to consciously create settings of enhanced social connection. One such example studied in *Hope under Neoliberal Austerity: Responses from civil society and civic universities* (2021) was that of a community café in the town of Chester-le-Street in north-east England. The café collects 'safe for consumption' surplus food from local shops and manufacturers and then offers this as meals and snacks to customers who 'pay as you feel'. This approach prevents food wastage, offers good food for low payment, and provides a social space within which people can connect and meet. This seems to be an excellent example of care in a commons context. Key concepts animating this project are 'quiet politics' and reciprocity. Quiet politics refers to the implicit actions which result from these new relational encounters. Through the 'asymmetrical reciprocity' involved differences can be respected 'through dialogue, encounters and interactions with others ...'[119] The café has had a significant impact on those who use it, with one participant speaking of the feeling of belonging to a community centred on the café. Her accounts reflect how '[r]elationality becomes both a personal and political tool in austerity' and its survival.[120]

Finding means and mechanisms to create new relational spaces offering a practical support and solidarity that go beyond the mere utilitarian and beyond the increasingly fragmented and displaced workplace will be crucial in mobilising the caring commons that we will need in the decades to come. Here again, the UBI mechanism liberates people's time to engage in community activity, frees them from the drudgery and oppression of precarious low-paid employment, and mobilises financial resources for them to build social connection.

4. *Releases commons creativity*

Finally, the UBI proposal, precisely by freeing people from the constraints outlined above, permits them to engage in work and tasks which they really wish to do. We are back in *The Hologram*'s utopian realm of time as a subversive resource where what you genuinely wish for becomes at least a somewhat more realisable possibility. What might people do when freed from economic pressure? What might they in fact wish for and then bring about? This is the exciting horizon of opportunity opened up by UBI through which the caring commons can come back into life.

My *Feasta*[121] colleague Anne Ryan has helpfully listed what citizen-leaders and pioneers (commoners in all but name) are already doing, even in the absence of UBI, to transform our social world and build our shared commons.[122] She organises these actions into four categories:

Critique
Showing what is wrong with the current system, resistance, protest and striking are all part of this work. It includes writing, podcasting, artistic work, popular education, and refusing jobs and other paid work that are personally, socially or ecologically harmful.

Creating
This is about making the new economy and culture through hands-on projects and enterprises. Examples are: transition towns; co-operative energy projects, seed banks, pollinator-friendly ecosystems, different kinds of land management and cultivation like agroforestry and all kinds of ecological agriculture; land reform movements; community-supported business models for farms, shops, breweries, bakeries and other enterprises; zero-waste initiatives; local currencies and exchange and trading systems; sustainable/ecological construction; creative commons; co-production in the arts; shared childcare; local repair and maintenance facilities; tool libraries; developing genuine indicators of progress; slow food, Cittaslow;[123] popular education for a culture shift; activism for democratic money; campaigning to cap fossil-fuel use; campaigning for just and ecological taxation systems; basic income campaigns; training and skills development.

Renewing
This includes reproducing and supporting what is good in the current system or what has recently disappeared

or is under threat in the local and community economy: small or medium farms delivering good food with low environmental impact; village shops and cafés; food and agriculture co-ops; credit unions; libraries; childcare, sick-care, elder-care and self-care; community education; gardening, allotments and grow-it-yourself; cooking and preserving skills; repair services; housing co-ops; working shorter job hours; community arts; playgroups; book clubs.

Coping
This work is largely concerned with supporting people, social systems, animal populations and ecosystems that have been damaged by the present economy and society. It ranges from surviving to hospicing, to healing and repairing; alleviating inequalities and suffering. It includes mental wellness groups; supporting refugees; bibliotherapy; men's sheds; animal rescue; community gardens; forest and woodland therapy; habitat restoration; rebuilding ecological and social systems; litter clean-ups; invasive plant management; walking, running and other exercise groups.

This list well evokes the texture and feel of our commons and points to how wide and transformative are the opportunities before us. Freed from economic dependence, individuals can embrace genuine lifelong learning and engage in the work of realising new modes of connection and thus of care.

Conclusion

The image of a caring Ireland presented here centres on a reformed dialogical system of social and health care and a welfare system grounded in a UBI. These combine to re-situate the enclosed self away from systems that foster passivity, dependency and compliance, into the new dynamic of the commoning self. The commoning self is called into being by these changes and is also supported with sufficient economic capacity to engage willingly in the work of connection. Not all will do so of course. However, the material necessity for care will act as the social glue drawing people together in mutual co-operation and support. While the professional care and health systems will be needed to perform complex and specialised tasks, they would do so in a new, inter-subjective, dialogical manner. Such a dialogical, co-produced model of formal care becomes compatible with, and demanded by, newly resourced commoning subjects.

This image is offered as an example of what is possible. While this is a hopeful and indeed positive picture of care in a new Ireland, at the end though we must acknowledge the hard and yet ennobling reality that care imposes limits, and limits means sacrifice. Such a recognition brings to the fore an old nuance in the traditional meaning of care as a burden which must be borne. Care requires giving time and attention to another. It requires losing part of myself and my will and my projects and my pleasure. The very corporeality of care – of my own body, the body of another, the physical world about me – interpolates the neoliberal subject and summons them back from subjective enclosure into the commons. Reconnecting with this framework of meaning as something essentially human is crucial for the mobilisation of our shared commons of care. Care is not a lost *eros* (freedom abandoned) but a re-discovered *agape* (conviviality recovered). To borrow in part from Tronto – the good life is not one that is carefree but rather care-filled.

Notes and References

All URL links were accessible at time of publication

1. http://www.census.nationalarchives.ie/pages/1901/Mayo/ Castlebar_Urban/Knockaphunta/1584335.

2. M. Foucault, 'The Order of Discourse', in R. Young (ed.), *Untying the Text: A post-structuralist reader* (Boston, London and Henley: Routledge & Kegan Paul, 1981), pp. 48–78.

3. M.L. de Souza, '"Sacrifice Zone": The environment–territory– place of disposable lives', *Community Development Journal*, vol. 56, no. 2, 2021, pp. 220–43.

4. It should be emphasised that this book's focus is the care *system* rather than specific instances of care *issues* in Ireland such as homelessness, direct provision, addiction, poverty, abortion, suicide, mental and physical health, Traveller rights, and so on.

5. I am not entering the wider debate about the validity or otherwise of characterising today's dominant economic system as 'neoliberal'. For my purposes in this book, the neoliberal signifier serves because it functions ideologically to frame what is regarded as meaningful and rational, and is the theoretical discourse underpinning the architecture of the care system.

6. https://www.irishtimes.com/health/2023/05/13/more-than-830000-patients-on-hospital-waiting-lists-last-month-figures-show.

7. https://www.rte.ie/news/health/2023/0214/1356614-hospitals.

8. https://www.rte.ie/news/2022/0615/1304871-ed-waiting-times.

9. https://www.rte.ie/news/health/2023/0831/1402556-camhs-reports.

10. https://www.rte.ie/news/ireland/2022/0523/1300631-camhs-delays.

11. https://www.thejournal.ie/delayed-delivery-survey-5707412-Mar2022.

12. https://www.cso.ie/en/census/census2016reports.

13. https://www.esri.ie/system/files/publications/RS144.pdf.

14. See, for example, http://www.rte.ie/news/2022/0626/1306886-childrens-disability-services.

15. See M. Power and C. Burke, 'Recruitment and Retention in Social Care Work in Ireland', 2021, available at: https://socialcareireland.ie/wp-content/uploads/2021/10/Recruitment-and-retention-report-SCI-1.pdf.

16. See, for example, https://www.rte.ie/news/health/2023/0413/1376703-imo-agm.

17. For an interesting treatment on this, see S. Junger, *Tribe: On homecoming and belonging* (London: Fourth Estate, 2017).

18. See, for example, D. Grossman, *On Killing: The psychological cost of learning to kill in war and society* (New York: Open Road Media, 2014).

19. J.C. Tronto, *Moral Boundaries: A political argument for an ethic of care* (New York and London: Routledge, 1993), p. 103.

20. Ibid., p. 106.

21. Ibid.

22. Ibid., p. 107.

23. Ibid.

24. M.P. de la Bellacasa, *Matters of Care: Speculative ethics in more than human worlds* (Minneapolis and London: University of Minnesota Press, 2017), p. 161.

25. A. Chatzidakis, J. Hakim, J. Litter and C. Rottenberg, *The Care Manifesto: The politics of interdependence* (London and New York: Verso, 2020).

26. M. Garavan, *Compassionate Activism* (Dublin: Peter Lang, 2012), p. 41.

27. A. Naess, *Ecology, Community and Lifestyle: Outline of an ecosophy* (Cambridge: Cambridge University Press, 1990).

28. For information on this, see http://trialogue.co.

29. Examples include housing qualification limits, means-testing as a norm, and reductions in jobseeker's allowance for the under-21s.

30. See R. Hearne, *Housing Shock* (Bristol: Policy Press, 2020).

31. See, for example, Inclusion Ireland, *The Distant Voice: A working paper on the first 50 Health Information and Quality Authority (HIQA) inspections of residential services for people with disabilities*, available at: https://inclusionireland.ie/wp-content/uploads/2020/11/thedistantvoice.pdf. See also https://villagemagazine.ie/turmoil-over-de-institutionalisation.

32. https://www.cso.ie/en/releasesandpublications/ep/p-silc/surveyonincomeandlivingconditionssilc2022.

33. See, for example, K. Pickett and R. Wilkinson, *The Spirit Level: Why more equal societies almost always do better* (London: Allen Lane, 2009).

34. R.D. Putnam, *Bowling Alone: The collapse and revival of American community* (New York: Simon & Schuster, 2000).

35. https://www.cso.ie/en/releasesandpublications/ep/p-tah/tenureandhouseholdsinireland2016–2019/demography.

36. M. Mulkeen, 'Care and the Standards of Proficiency for Social Care Workers', *Irish Journal of Applied Social Studies*, vol. 20, no. 2, 2020, p. 21, available at: https://arrow.tudublin.ie/ijass/vol20/iss2/4.

37. J. Harris, '(Against) Neoliberal Social Work', *Critical and Radical Social Work*, vol. 2, no. 1, 2014, p. 9.

38. Ibid., p. 16.

39. Rank and yank refers to performance systems that first rank workers according to compliance and output determined by the performance metrics and then 'yank' or fire those not performing adequately. Some US companies had applications of this whereby the bottom 10 per cent of staff were automatically fired. It is easy to see in this context how workers would respond with compliance.

40. P. Verhaeghe, *What About Me? The struggle for identity in a market-based society* (Victoria and London: Scribe, 2014), p. 139.

41. Ibid., pp. 134–5.

42. The 2021 UK report *Workforce Burnout and Resilience in the NHS and Social Care* reported that:

The NHS Staff Survey has suggested that an unacceptably high proportion of NHS staff experience negative impacts as a result of stress in the workplace and that the proportion of staff suffering from stress is on an upward trend. The 2019 survey found that 40.3% of respondents reported feeling unwell as a result of work-related stress in the last 12 months, up from 36.8% in 2016. The most recent iteration of the survey, where fieldwork took place during the pandemic, indicated that 44% of respondents have now reported feeling unwell as a result of work-related stress in the last 12 months. The latest survey also found that 46.4% of staff said that they had gone to work in the last three months despite not feeling well enough to perform their duties – although this was 'notably fewer' than in previous years (2021, pp. 2–14).

43. R. Salecl, 'Choice and the Ultimate Incurable', *Umbr(a): Incurable*, no. 1, 2006, p. 85.

44. R. Salecl, *The Tyranny of Choice* (London: Profile Books, 2010), p. 31.

45. Ibid., p. 148.

46. See N. Rose, *Governing the Soul: The shaping of the private self* (London: Taylor & Francis/Routledge, 1990).

47. See S. Zuboff, *The Age of Surveillance Capitalism: The fight for a human future at the new frontier of power* (London: Profile Books, 2019).

48. To see a left critique of the implications of these forms of identity politics, see, for example, V. Chibber, *The Class Matrix: Social theory after the cultural turn* (Cambridge, MA: Harvard University Press, 2022).

49. J. Lanier, *You Are Not a Gadget: A manifesto* (London: Penguin, 2011), p. xiii.

50. Ibid., p. 20.

51. J. Sinclair, 'Don't Mourn for Us', *Our Voice*, vol. 1, no. 3, 1993.

52. In outlining these ideas on dialogue I am drawing from my article 'Dialogic Practice in Social Work: Towards a renewed humanistic method', *Journal of Social Intervention: Theory and practice*, vol. 1, no. 22, 2013, pp. 4–20.

53. J. Seikkula and D. Trimble, 'Healing Elements of Therapeutic Conversation: Dialogue as an embodiment of love', *Family Process*, vol. 44, no. 4, 2005, p. 465.

54. M. Bakhtin, *Speech Genres and Other Late Essays* (Austin, TX: University of Texas Press, 1986), p. 127.

55. See, for example, S. Malloch and C. Trevarthen, *Communicative Musicality: Exploring the basis of human companionship* (Oxford: Oxford University Press, 2009).

56. M. Buber, *I and Thou* (Edinburgh: T. & T. Clark Ltd., 1984), p. 62.

57. Bakhtin, *Speech Genres*, p. 293.

58. J. Seikkula, 'Becoming Dialogical: Psychotherapy or a way of life?', *The Australian and New Zealand Journal of Family Therapy*, vol. 32, no. 3, 2011, p. 185.

59. P. Freire, *Pedagogy of the Oppressed* (London: Penguin Books, 1986), p. 99.

60. Ibid., p. 61.

61. Seikkula, 'Becoming Dialogical', p. 184.

62. See, for example, J. Seikkula et al., 'The Comprehensive Open-Dialogue Approach in Western Lapland: II. Long-term stability of acute psychosis outcomes in advanced community care', *Psychosis*, vol. 3, no. 3, 2011, pp. 1–13.

63. https://www.buurtzorg.com/about-us/buurtzorgmodel.

64. See M. Slade, L. Oades and A. Jarden (eds), *Wellbeing, Recovery and Mental Health* (Cambridge: Cambridge University Press, 2017); J. Repper, 'Adjusting the Focus of Mental Health Nursing: Incorporating service users' experiences of

recovery', *Journal of Mental Health*, vol. 9, no. 6, 2000, pp. 575–87; J. Read, L.R. Mosher and R.P. Bentall (eds), *Models of Madness: Psychological, social and biological approaches to schizophrenia* (Hove and New York: Routledge, 2004).

65. https://www.gmit.ie/certificate-in-peer-support-practice; https://www.dcu.ie/courses/undergraduate/school-nursing-psychotherapy-and-community-health/certificate-peer-support.

66. https://www.recoverycollegewest.ie/mayo.

67. I wish to acknowledge the initial suggestion regarding *The Hologram* and general inspiration received from the independent care activist Thom Stewart.

68. C. Thornton, *The Hologram: Feminist, peer-to-peer health for a post-pandemic future* (London: Pluto Press, 2020), p. xvii.

69. Ibid., p. xiv.

70. Ibid., p. 5.

71. Ibid., p. 8.

72. Ibid., p. 10.

73. Ibid., p. 6.

74. Ibid., p. 13.

75. See, for example, https://equalitytrust.org.uk/resource/paul-piff-social-trust.

76. Thornton, *The Hologram*, pp. 16–17.

77. Ibid., p. 17.

78. Consider here the Lacanian observation that desire is the desire of the other, and Girard's work on the mimetic nature of desire.

79. Thornton, *The Hologram*, pp. 23–4.

80. Ibid., p. 27.

81. Ibid., pp. 27–8.

82. Ibid., p. 31.

83. See Rudolf Bahro's notion of 'liberated spaces'. Also,

the discussion of the *zone à défendre* in Z. Ahmad et al., 'Environmentalism from the margins: Interviews with scholar-activists', *Community Development Journal*, vol. 57, no. 1, 2022, pp. 132–66.

84. Thornton, *The Hologram*, p. 35.

85. Ibid., p. 36.

86. Ibid., p. 51.

87. Ibid.

88. For a short illustration, see https://www.youtube.com/watch?v=x8HbXR4A4yk&t=11s.

89. Thornton, *The Hologram*, p. 97.

90. Ibid., p. 99.

91. Ibid., p. 100.

92. Ibid., pp. 104–5.

93. According to Carl Rogers, 'Good communication, free communication, with or between men, is always therapeutic.' *On Becoming a Person: A therapist's view of psychotherapy* (London: Constable, 1989), p. 333.

94. See E. Ward, *Self* (Cork: Cork University Press, 2021), especially pp. 43–67.

95. See *The Mental State of the World in 2022*, p. 2: 'The most dramatic decline from older to younger generations has been along the dimension of the Social Self, a metric of the way we see ourselves and our ability to form and maintain relationships with others. In 2022 we probed the state of family relationships and friendships and highlight here their progressive degradation over generations as one driving factor. Younger adults report increasingly higher rates of family instability and conflict and lack of love and emotional warmth during childhood, despite growing rates of material support by their parents and investment in their accomplishments. They are also three times more likely to have poor adult family relationships compared to their parents' generation and twice as likely to lack friends who will help them in times of need. Poignantly, those with

poor family relationships and no close friends are ten times more likely to suffer from significant mental health challenges than those with many close family bonds and friendships. These data suggest that we have not fully appreciated the profoundly relational nature of the human psyche. Importantly, it invites each of us to reflect on our role in the growing social disintegration. What have we valued and why? Where have we focused our attention? And with finite time, just how much have we cast aside an active commitment to love or social nurturing for material success or even just mindless scrolling of the Internet? We can't change the past, but with some collective reflection perhaps we can change how it plays out for future generations.' Available at: https://mentalstateoftheworld.report.

96. K. Lynch, *Care and Capitalism: Why affective equality matters for social justice* (London: Polity Press, 2022), pp. 3–4.

97. G. Esteva, 'Commoning in the New Society', *Community Development Journal*, vol. 49, no. 1, 2014, p. 148.

98. Ibid., p. 156.

99. J. Tronto, *Caring Democracy: Markets, equality, and justice* (New York: New York University Press, 2013), p. xv.

100. Ibid., p. 170.

101. Ibid., p. 178.

102. The question of financially recognising domestic labour has a long history in feminist thought and activism. Note, for example, the International Wages for Housework Campaign dating from the early 1970s. See L. Toupin, *Wages for Housework* (London: Pluto Press, 2018). More recently, see initiatives such as 'The Wellbeing Economy' (https://weall.org), which is exploring questions of economic equality in a new, participative economy. Its Irish hub can be accessed at: https://weall.org/hub/ireland. There is growing scholarly attention on the concept of de-growth which includes a renewed focus on the domestic space as a site of commons labour. See, for example, C. Dengler and B. Strunk, 'The Monetized Economy Versus Care and the Environment: Degrowth perspectives on reconciling an antagonism', *Feminist Economics*, vol. 24, no. 3, 2017, pp. 160–83;

T. Parrique, 'Degrowth', in *Handbook of the Anthropocene: Humans between heritage and future* (Cham: Springer International Publishing, 2023), pp. 1113–17; see also https://www. degrowthjournal.org/issues/2023-volume-1.

103. For comprehensive treatments of recovering the value of the commons, see A. McKay, *The Future of Social Security Policy: Women, work and a citizen's basic income* (London and New York: Routledge, 2005); S. Federici, *Re-enchanting the World: Feminism and the politics of the commons* (Oakland, CA: PM Press, 2019).

104. J. Pieper, *Faith, Hope, Love*, trans. Richard and Clara Winston (San Francisco: Ignatius Press, 1997), p. 164. See also the affirmation therapy proposed by Conrad Baars in, for example, C. Baars, *Born only Once: The Miracle of Affirmation* (Eugene, Oregon: WIPF & Stock, 2016, 3rd Edition).

105. See Mel Baggs, 'In My Language', available at: https:// www.youtube.com/watch?v=JnylM1hI2jc; G. Thomas, *Disability, Normalcy, and the Everyday* (London: Routledge, 2018); J.M. Reynolds, *The Life Worth Living: Disability, pain, and morality* (Minneapolis: University of Minnesota Press, 2022); R. Michalko, *The Difference that Disability Makes* (Philadelphia: Temple University Press, 2002).

106. For more, see https://planetyouth.ie.

107. See https://basicincome.ie.

108. To recognise how UBI is not a particularly outlandish proposal politically, note that a commitment to trialling it is in the Programme for Government of the Fine Gael, Fianna Fáil and Green Party administration which took office in 2020; universal payments were made to workers made unemployed during Covid restrictions; and the current government has also introduced a basic income support for 2,000 artists for three years on a trial basis beginning in 2022.

109. P. Van Parijs and Y. Vanderborght, *Basic Income: A radical proposal for a free society and a sane economy* (Cambridge, MA: Harvard University Press, 2017).

110. Ibid., p. 10.

111. https://data.oecd.org/ireland.htm.

112. Calculated with exchange rates on 1 September 2023.

113. Van Parijs and Vanderborght, *Basic Income*, p. 16.

114. D. Graeber, *Bullshit Jobs: A theory* (London: Allen Lane, 2018).

115. See, for example, D.J. Siegel, *The Developing Mind: How relationships and the brain interact to shape who we are* (London and New York: Guilford Press, 2020).

116. M. Ward et al., 'Loneliness, Social Isolation, and their Discordance among Older Adults', findings from The Irish Longitudinal Study on Ageing (TILDA), available at: http://www.tara.tcd.ie/handle/2262/89853.

117. https://www.tasc.ie/assets/files/pdf/2308-1_tasc_feps_mental_health_report-final.pdf.

118. R. Bregman, *Humankind: A hopeful history* (London: Bloomsbury Publishing, 2020), p. 304.

119. J. Midgley and S. Slather, 'Café Society: Transforming community through quiet activism and reciprocity', in M. Steer et al. (eds), *Hope under Neoliberal Austerity: Responses from civil society and civic universities* (Bristol: Policy Press, 2021), p. 75.

120. Ibid., p. 84.

121. See www.feasta.org and more specifically https://www.feasta.org/category/basic-income.

122. A. Ryan, 'Basic Income Now: A high-leverage system intervention for sanity, humanity and ecology', July 2019, available at: https://www.feasta.org/2019/07/22/basic-income-now-a-high-leverage-system-intervention-for-sanity-humanity-and-ecology.

123. See https://www.cittaslow.org/content/our-principles.

Bibliography

Ahmad, Z. et al., 'Reflections: Environmentalism from the margins. Interviews with scholar-activists', *Community Development Journal*, vol. 57, no. 1, 2022, pp. 132–66

Bakhtin, M., *Speech Genres and Other Late Essays* (Austin, TX: University of Texas Press, 1986)

Bellacasa, M.P. de la, *Matters of Care: Speculative ethics in more than human worlds* (Minneapolis and London: University of Minnesota Press, 2017)

Bregman, R., *Humankind: A hopeful history* (London: Bloomsbury Publishing, 2020)

Buber, M., *I and Thou* (Edinburg: T. & T. Clark Ltd., 1984)

Chatzidakis, A., J. Hakim, J. Litter and C. Rottenberg, *The Care Manifesto: The politics of interdependence* (London and New York: Verso, 2020)

Chibber, V., *The Class Matrix: Social theory after the cultural turn* (Cambridge, MA: Harvard University Press, 2022)

Dengler C. and B. Strunk, 'The Monetized Economy Versus Care and the Environment: Degrowth perspectives on reconciling an antagonism', *Feminist Economics*, vol. 24, no. 3, 2017, pp. 160–83

Ehrenreich, B., *Smile or Die: How positive thinking fooled America and the world* (London: Granta, 2010)

Esteva, G., 'Commoning in the New Society', *Community Development Journal*, vol. 49, no. 1, 2014, pp. 144–59

Federici, F., *Re-enchanting the World: Feminism and the politics of the commons* (Oakland, CA: PM Press, 2019)

Foucault, M., 'The Order of Discourse', in R. Young (ed.), *Untying the Text: A post-structuralist reader* (Boston, London and Henley: Routledge & Kegan Paul, 1981), pp. 48–78

Freire, P., *Pedagogy of the Oppressed* (London: Penguin Books, 1986)

Garavan, M., *Compassionate Activism* (Dublin: Peter Lang, 2012)

———, 'Dialogic Practice in Social Work: Towards a renewed humanistic method', *Journal of Social Intervention: Theory and practice*, vol. 1, no. 22, 2013, pp. 4–20

Girard, R., *Deceit, Desire, and the Novel: Self and other in literary structure* (Baltimore and London: The Johns Hopkins University Press, 1976)

Graeber, D., *Bullshit Jobs: A theory* (London: Allen Lane, 2018)

Grossman, D., *On Killing: The psychological cost of learning to kill in war and society* (New York: Open Road Media, 2014)

Harris, J., '(Against) Neoliberal Social Work', *Critical and Radical Social Work*, vol. 2, no. 1, 2014, pp. 7–22

———, *The Social Work Business* (London: Routledge, 2002)

Hearne, R., *Housing Shock* (Bristol: Policy Press, 2020)

Inclusion Ireland, *The Distant Voice: A working paper on the first 50 Health Information and Quality Authority (HIQA) inspections of residential services for people with disabilities*, available at: https://inclusionireland.ie/wp-content/uploads/2020/11/thedistantvoice.pdf

Junger, S., *Tribe: On homecoming and belonging* (London: Fourth Estate, 2017)

Lanier, J., *You Are Not a Gadget: A manifesto* (London: Penguin, 2011)

Lynch, K., *Care and Capitalism: Why affective equality matters for social justice* (London: Polity Press, 2022)

Malloch, S. and C. Trevarthen, *Communicative Musicality: Exploring the basis of human companionship* (Oxford: Oxford University Press, 2009)

McKay, A., *The Future of Social Security Policy: Women, work and a citizens' basic income* (London and New York: Routledge, 2005)

Michalko, R., *The Difference that Disability Makes* (Philadelphia: Temple University Press, 2002)

Midgley, J. and S. Slather, 'Café Society: Transforming community through quiet activism and reciprocity', in M. Steer et al. (eds), *Hope under Neoliberal Austerity: Responses from civil society and civic universities* (Bristol: Policy Press, 2021), pp. 73–88

Mulkeen, M., 'Care and the Standards of Proficiency for Social Care Workers', *Irish Journal of Applied Social Studies*, vol. 20, no. 2, Article 4, available at: https://arrow.tudublin.ie/ijass/vol20/iss2/4

Naess, A., *Ecology, Community and Lifestyle: Outline of an ecosophy* (Cambridge: Cambridge University Press, 1990)

Parrique, T., 'Degrowth', in *Handbook of the Anthropocene: Humans between heritage and future* (Cham: Springer International Publishing, 2023), pp. 1113–17

Pickett, K. and R. Wilkinson, *The Spirit Level: Why more equal societies almost always do better* (London: Allen Lane, 2009)

Pieper, J., *Faith, Hope, Love*, trans. Richard and Clara Winston (San Francisco: Ignatius Press, 1997)

Power, M. and C. Burke, 'Recruitment and Retention in Social Care Work in Ireland', 2021, available at: https://socialcareireland.ie/wp-content/uploads/2021/10/Recruitment-and-retention-report-SCI-1.pdf

Putnam, R.D., *Bowling Alone: The collapse and revival of American community* (New York: Simon & Schuster, 2000)

Read, J., L.R. Mosher and R.P. Bentall (eds), *Models of Madness: Psychological, social and biological approaches to schizophrenia* (Hove and New York: Routledge, 2004)

Repper, J., 'Adjusting the Focus of Mental Health Nursing: Incorporating service users' experiences of recovery', *Journal of Mental Health*, vol. 9, no. 6, 2000, pp. 575–87

Reynolds, J.M., *The Life Worth Living: Disability, pain, and morality* (Minneapolis: University of Minnesota Press, 2022)

Ritzer, G., *The McDonaldization of Society* (California: Pine Forge Press, 2011)

Rogers, C., *On Becoming a Person: A therapist's view of psychotherapy* (London: Constable, 1989)

Rose, N., *Governing the Soul: The shaping of the private self* (London: Taylor & Francis/Routledge, 1990)

Ryan, A., 'Basic Income Now: A high-leverage system intervention for sanity, humanity and ecology', July 2019, available at: https://www.feasta.org/2019/07/22/basic-income-now-a-high-leverage-system-intervention-for-sanity-humanity-and-ecology/

Salecl, R., 'Choice and the Ultimate Incurable', *Umbr(a): Incurable*, no. 1, 2006, pp. 85–98

———, *The Tyranny of Choice* (London: Profile Books, 2010)

Seikkula, J., 'Becoming Dialogical: Psychotherapy or a way of life?', *The Australian and New Zealand Journal of Family Therapy*, vol. 32, no. 3, 2011, pp. 179–93

Seikkula, J. and D. Trimble, 'Healing Elements of Therapeutic Conversation: Dialogue as an embodiment of love', *Family Process*, vol. 44, no. 4, 2005, pp. 461–75

Seikkula, J. and T.E. Arnkil, *Dialogical Meetings in Social Networks* (London and New York: Karnac, 2006)

Seikkula, J. et al., 'The Comprehensive Open-Dialogue Approach in Western Lapland: II. Long-term stability of acute psychosis outcomes in advanced community care', *Psychosis*, vol. 3, no. 3, 2011, pp. 1–13

Siegel, D.J., *The Developing Mind: How relationships and the brain interact to shape who we are* (London and New York: Guilford Press, 2020)

Sinclair, J., 'Don't Mourn for Us', *Our Voice*, vol. 1, no. 3, 1993

Slade, M., L. Oades and A. Jarden (eds), *Wellbeing, Recovery and Mental Health* (Cambridge: Cambridge University Press, 2017)

Souza, M.L., de, '"Sacrifice Zone": The environment–territory–place of disposable lives', *Community Development Journal*, vol. 56, no. 2, 2021, pp. 220–43

The Mental State of the World in 2022, available at: https://mentalstateoftheworld.report/

Thomas, G., *Disability, Normalcy, and the Everyday* (London: Routledge, 2018)

Thornton, C., *The Hologram: Feminist, peer-to-peer health for a post-pandemic future* (London: Pluto Press, 2020)

Toupin, L., translated by Käthe Roth, *Wages for Housework: A history of an international feminist movement, 1972–77* (London: Pluto Press, 2018)

Tronto, J.C., *Caring Democracy: Markets, equality, and justice* (New York: New York University Press, 2013)

———, *Moral Boundaries: A political argument for an ethic of care* (New York and London: Routledge, 1993)

Van Parijs, P. and Y. Vanderborght, *Basic Income: A radical proposal for a free society and a sane economy* (Cambridge, MA: Harvard University Press, 2017)

Verhaeghe, P., *What About Me? The struggle for identity in a market-based society* (Victoria and London: Scribe, 2014)

Ward, E., *Self* (Cork: Cork University Press, 2021)

Ward, M. et al., 'Loneliness, Social Isolation, and their Discordance among Older Adults', findings from The Irish Longitudinal Study on Ageing (TILDA), available at: http://www.tara.tcd.ie/handle/2262/89853

Žižek, S., *How to Read Lacan* (London: Granta Books, 2006)

Zuboff, S., *The Age of Surveillance Capitalism: The fight for a human future at the new frontier of power* (London: Profile Books, 2019)

Index